APPLIED BIOCHEMISTRY FOR B.SC NURSING STUDENTS

ACCORDING TO INC SYLLABUS

RACHNA MAAN SINGH

To

Dear GOD

My Father and mother

For leading their children into Intellectual Pursuits

Contents

Preface

The title of this book adequately indicate its scope in the field of nursing and is concerned with the base of biochemistry on which nursing practice is built.

this book is designed according to the INC syllabus , to help students in their exam preperation and every topic is covered in this book which is provided in B.Sc Nursing syllabus .

The salient features of the book are:

- Simple Language
- Easy to Understand
- As per INC sylllabus

suggestions from the nursing lecturers as well as from the students will be duly acknowledged.

Acknowledgements

I would like to thank my parents , without their continues support , i will not able to complete this project. I appreciate college in which i am working (Prem Institute of Medical Sciences) for providing me time and dedication to complete this book. In last I warmly thank my readers. I hope this book will help you understand the basic concepts of Biochemsistry .

Rachna Maan Singh
Assistant Professor
Prem Institute of Medical Sciences, Panipat

CHAPTER I

Carbohydrates

Carbohydrates

- Digestion, absorption and metabolism of carbohydrates and related disorders
- Regulation of blood glucose
- Diabetes Mellitus - type 1 & type 2, symptoms, complications & management in brief
- Investigations of Diabetes Mellitus
    - OGTT: Indications, Procedure, Interpretation and types of GTT curve
    - Mini GTT, extended GTT, GCT, IV GTT
    - HbA1c (Only definition)
- Hypoglycemia-definition & causes

Digestion, absorption and metabolism of carbohydrates and related disorders

Digestion

Digestion is the procedure of breaking down large, insoluble food molecules into smaller blood vessels to take in them into the bloodstream. This method involves the use of large quantities of digestive juices and enzymes which includes saliva, mucus, bile, and hydrochloric acid, among others.

There are four main stages of digestion in the human body:

• After eating food, it passes through the stomach to the small intestine, wherein it's miles digested.

• vitamins from digested food enter the bloodstream via small holes within the small intestine.

• Unprocessed leftover meals is sent to the massive intestine, in which any untreated water or vitamins are re-delivered into the frame.

- The residual waste products from the body are excreted

Absorption

Absorption is the process of soaking up or absorbing material from cells or all tissues and organs via the system of distribution or osmosis.

Digestion and Absorption of Carbohydrates

Carbohydrates are one of the maximum important nutrients within the human eating regimen. There are two kinds of carbohydrates that can be digested by using the human digestive device - sugar and starch.

Sugar is reduced inside the small gut and 3 oral enzymes, namely Lactase, Sucrase, and Maltase.

In a comparable manner, starch is broken down with the assist of Amylase enzymes present inside the mouth and stomach. After digestion, carbohydrates are absorbed into the small gut with the assist of tiny finger-like structures called Villi.

Carbohydrate metabolism

dietary glucose is located in abundance in starch. Amalyse enzymes lessen starch to aid metabolism. Glucose consists of many resources inclusive of lactose (from milk), fructose (from fruit), and sucrose (desk sugar). functional membrane systems facilitate the absorption of fructose, glucose, and fructose referred to as monosaccharide species. Monosaccharide fractions are fashioned with the aid of the separation of disaccharides with the aid of unique intestinal glucosidase. kinds of glucose along with maltose are hydrolyzed by isomaltose with minimum ability for preferred results. Lactose intolerance is resulting from a deficiency of lactase - an enzyme needed to break down lactose into milk and different dairy merchandise.

The small intestine contains mucosal cells within the intestines that carry monosaccharides into the circulatory machine, where they progress to the liver. here, galactose and fructose are converted to glucose. The primary function of the liver is to adjust blood glucose degrees, or in other phrases, to function as a blood glucostat. excess glucose molecules are saved typically within the liver and muscle cells as glycogen. it is also stored in the shape of fats integrated into adipocytes. as opposed to fat, handiest glycogen may be used to preserve an adequate level of glucose inside the blood while food is confined. Oils can be used for oxidative regeneration of ATP and depleted electricity (NADH).

Carbohydrate disorders:-

Disruption of Carbohydrate Metabolism

mistaken carbohydrate metabolism can purpose many sicknesses. the following are a number of the maximum common ones -

Diabetes mellitus: happens because of insulin deficiency or resistance, main to hyper or hypoglycemia.

Lactose intolerance: basically, it's far a common hypersensitivity in adults. in the main it occurs because of a deficiency of the enzyme lactase. This enzyme is liable for the conversion of lactose disaccharides into glucose monosaccharides.

Galactosemia: This particular disorder is quite rare. It is caused due to congenital mutations in enzymes which are a part of glucose metabolic pathways.

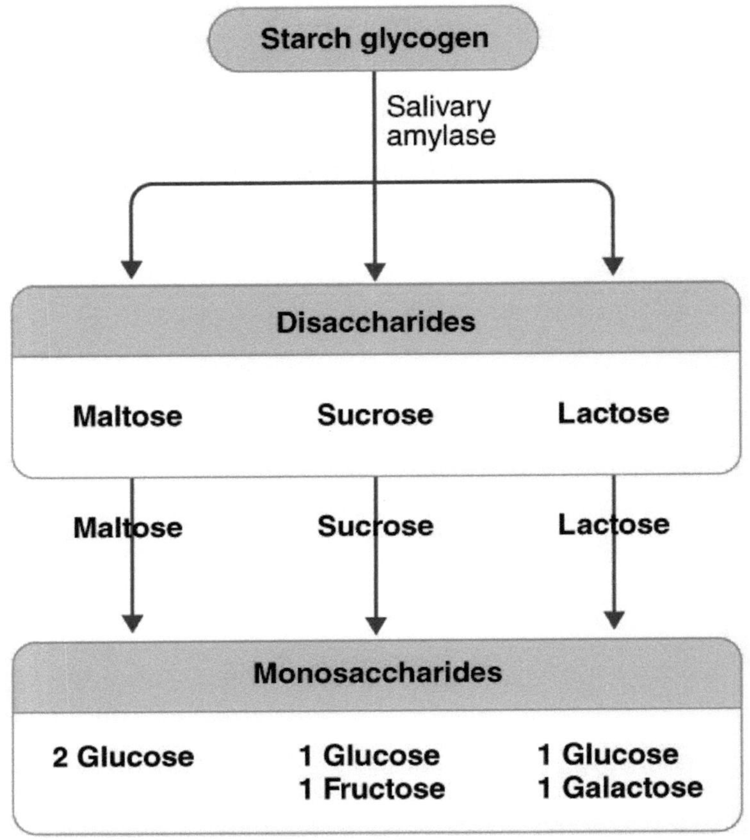

digestion and absorption of carbohydrates

Metabolism of carbohydrates

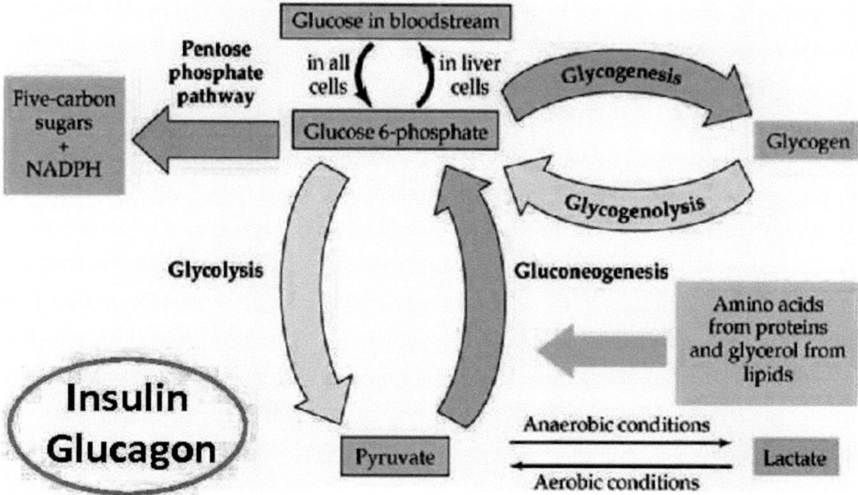

Metabolism of carbohydrates

Regulation of blood glucose

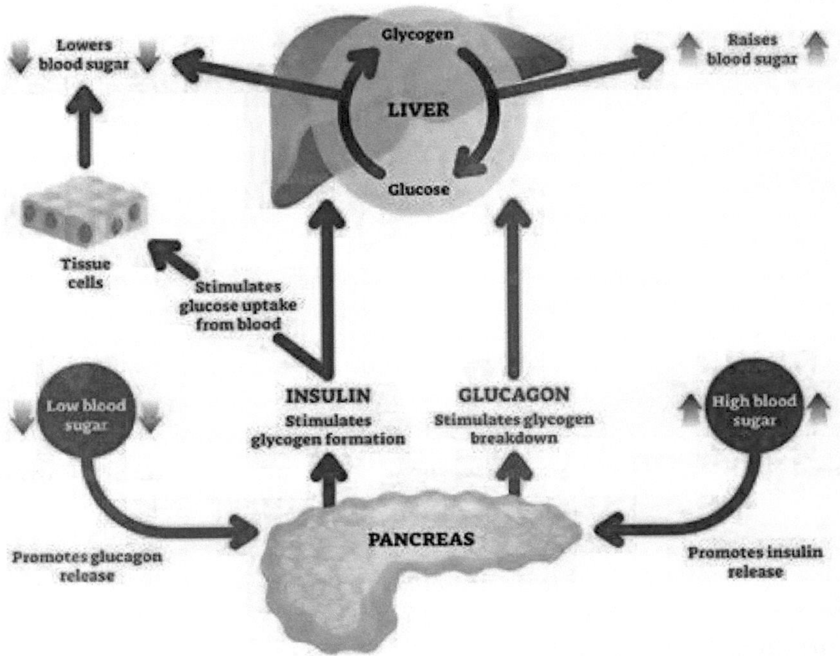

Control of blood glucose

Glucose manage inside the body is achieved mechanically and every minute of the day. normal BG stages have to be between 60 and 140mg / dL to provide the body cells with their required energy. brain cells do no longer want insulin to force glucose into neurons; however, there need to nevertheless be everyday expenses available. Too little sugar, known as **hypoglycemia**, hunger cells, and an excessive amount of sugar **(hyperglycemia)** creates a sticky, crippling effect on cells. Euglycemia, or hypoglycemia, is a natural reaction to physical hobby. A smooth stability is needed among hormones inside the pancreas, intestines, mind, or even the adrenals to hold ordinary BG stages.

Fuels of the Body

- To appreciate the pathology of diabetes, it is vital to apprehend how the body generally uses meals for energy. Glucose, fats, and proteins are the ingredients that fuel the body. understanding how the pancreatic, digestive, and intestinal hormones are involved in meals metabolism can help you apprehend everyday body structure and the way troubles increase with diabetes.
- All through the body, cells use glucose as a supply of immediate electricity. To preserve the frame going for walks smoothly, a non-stop awareness of 60 to one hundred mg/dL of glucose in blood plasma is wanted. in the course of workout or pressure the frame desires a higher concentration because muscle groups require glucose for power (Basu et al., 2009). Of the three fuels for the body, glucose is preferred as it produces both strength and water through the Krebs cycle and aerobic metabolism. The frame also can use protein and fats; however, their breakdown creates ketoacids, making the frame acidic, which isn't always its most effective kingdom. excess of ketoacids can produce metabolic acidosis.
- Functioning frame tissues constantly absorb glucose from the bloodstream. For individuals who do not have the diabetes, a meal of carbohydrates replenishes the circulating blood glucose about 10 mins after consuming and keeps until about 2 hours after ingesting. a first-section launch of insulin occurs approximately five mins after a meal and a second segment begins at about 20 mins. due to the fact the duration of insulin's impact is most effective approximately 2 hours, taking a 2-hour **postprandial** (after meal) BG suggests how well insulin became launched and used by the frame. The meals is broken down into small components together with glucose and is then absorbed through the intestines into the bloodstream. Glucose (ability strength) that is not at once used is stored through the body as glycogen inside the muscle mass, liver, and fats.
- The body is designed to live to tell the tale and so it shops electricity effectively, as fats. most individuals have excess fats due to the fact they fill up the glucose stores by consuming before any fat needs to be damaged down.
- when blood glucose levels fall after 2 hours, the liver replenishes the circulating blood glucose by using liberating glycogen (stored glucose). Glycogen is a polysaccharide, made and saved often in the cells of the liver. Glycogen gives an electricity reserve that can be quick mobilized

to meet a surprising need for glucose.

Hormones of the Pancreas

Regulation of blood glucose is largely carried out thru the endocrine hormones of the pancreas, a lovely stability of hormones carried out thru a bad feedback loop. the main hormones of the pancreas that affect blood glucose consist of insulin, glucagon, somatostatin, and amylin.

- Insulin (formed in pancreatic beta cells) lowers BG stages, whereas glucagon (from pancreatic alpha cells) elevates BG levels.Somatostatin is fashioned inside the delta cells of the pancreas and acts as the "pancreatic policeman," balancing insulin and glucagon. It allows the pancreas change in turning on or turning off every opposing hormone.
- Amylin is a hormone, made in a 1:one hundred ratio with insulin, that enables boom satiety, or satisfaction and nation of fullness from a meal, to prevent overeating. It additionally allows slow the belly contents from emptying too fast, to avoid a short spike in BG degrees.
- As a meal containing carbohydrates is eaten and digested, BG ranges rise, and the pancreas activates insulin manufacturing and turns off glucagon manufacturing. Glucose from the bloodstream enters liver cells, stimulating the movement of several enzymes that convert the glucose to chains of glycogen—so long as each insulin and glucose remain ample. on this postprandial or "fed" country, the liver takes in extra glucose from the blood than it releases. After a meal has been digested and BG degrees start to fall, insulin secretion drops and glycogen synthesis stops.
- whilst it's miles wished for energy, the liver breaks down glycogen and converts it to glucose for clean transport through the bloodstream to the cells of the frame.In a wholesome liver, up to ten% of its overall volume is used for glycogen shops. Skeletal muscle cells store about 1% of glycogen. The liver converts glycogen back to glucose whilst it's miles needed for electricity and regulates the quantity of glucose circulating among food.
- Your liver is high-quality in that it is aware of how a good deal to store and preserve, or damage down and launch, to hold best plasma glucose degrees. Imitation of this system is the goal of insulin remedy whilst glucose stages are controlled externally. Basal–bolus dosing is used as clinicians try and reflect this regular cycle.

- A wholesome body calls for a minimum concentration of circulating glucose (60 to 100 mg/dl), excessive continual concentrations motive health problems and are poisonous:
- **Acutely:** Hyperglycaemia of >300 mg/dl reasons polyuria, resulting in dehydration. Profound hyperglycaemia (>500 mg/dl) ends in confusion, cerebral oedema, coma, and, subsequently, dying (Ferrante, 2007).
- **Chronically**: Hyperglycaemia thataverages greater than 120 to 130 mg/dl progressively damages tissues throughout the frame and makes someone more liable to infections. The glucose will become syrupy within the bloodstream, intoxicating cells and competing with life-giving oxygen.

The concentration of glucose within the blood is determined by using the balance between the rate of glucose getting into and the price of glucose leaving the movement. these alerts are added at some point of the frame by two pancreatic hormones, insulin and glucagon (Maitra, 2009). choicest health requires that:

- While blood glucose concentrations are low, the liver is signaled to feature glucose to the stream.
- While blood glucose concentrations are excessive, the liver and the skeletal muscles are signaled to remove glucose from the move.

- **Diabetes Mellitus - type 1 & type 2, symptoms, complications & management in brief**

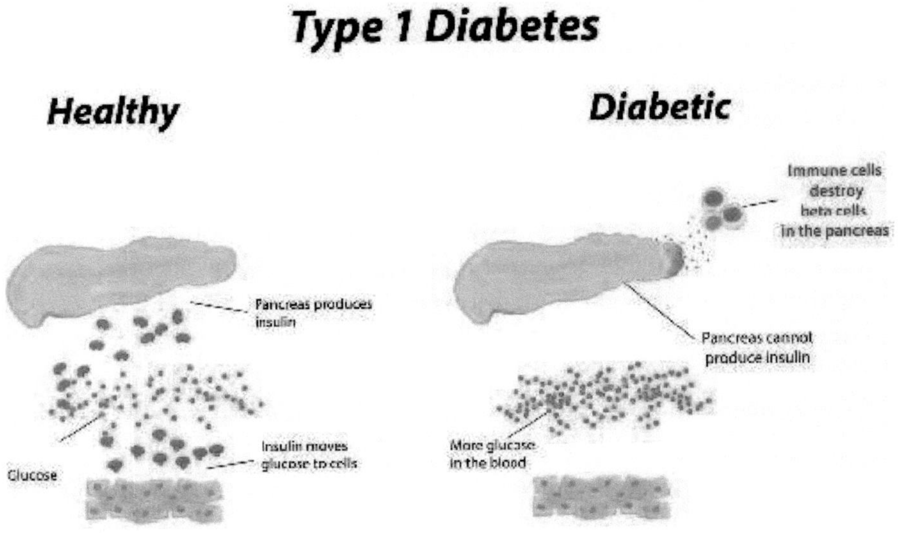

Type 1 Diabetes

Healthy **Diabetic**

Pancreas produces insulin
Insulin moves glucose to cells
Glucose
Immune cells destroy beta cells in the pancreas
Pancreas cannot produce insulin
More glucose in the blood

Diabetes mellitus type 1

Diabetes Mellitus Type 1 is the most intense form of diabetes, in which not sufficient insulin is produced by way of the body. the dearth of insulin effects in excessive blood sugar ranges.

Insulin is a hormone produced by means of the pancreas that allows your body to use glucose (a type of sugar determined in many carbohydrates) for strength. Insulin additionally helps to stability your blood glucose or blood sugar stages, with the aid of preventing it from getting too high (hyperglycemia) or too low (hypoglycemia)

CAUSES:-

The precise reason of kind 1 diabetes is unknown. health workers agree on the truth that this is an autoimmune condition in which the immune system of the body is mistakenly conditioned to attack and break the cells inside the pancreas, which produces the hormone insulin.

- Insulin enables to free up the cells of the frame to permit the sugar (glucose) to enter them so that the glucose is transformed into energy. If there's more sugar inside the frame than is required, the insulin helps to store the sugar inside the liver and releases it whilst the blood sugar stage is low, or whilst the frame needs greater sugar, which include in between food or during lively bodily activity. consequently, insulin facilitates to stability out the blood sugar level and maintain it in a everyday range. As blood sugar level will increase, the pancreas secretes greater insulin.

- Body does not produce enough insulin or the cells for your body are resistant to the results of insulin, you can expand hyperglycemia (high blood sugar). If the blood sugar ranges stay increased for lengthy durations of time it can lead to lengthy-time period headaches.
- In diabetes type 1, insulin does no longer get produced inside the frame. with out insulin, the cells are starved of strength, and the sugar ranges maintain rising within the blood.

Symptoms of high blood sugar or Diabetes Mellitus Type 1 include:

- excessive urination
- immoderate thirst
- surprising weight loss
- Fatigue
- accelerated hunger
- Blurry vision
- sluggish recovery wounds

Diagnosis

Diagnosis of diabetes type 1 usually includes one or more blood tests:

- Glycated haemoglobin (A1C) take a look at. This take a look at shows your blood sugar stages for the past two to three months. This test measures the share of haemoglobin — an oxygen-transporting protein in pink blood cells — to which the blood sugar is hooked up. A excessive percentage of haemoglobin (6.5 % or higher) indicates diabetes.
- Autoantibody test, which checks for antibodies that assault the pancreatic cells.
- Random Blood Sugar test
- Fasting Blood Sugar check and an Oral Glucose Tolerance check (OGTT).

The complications of diabetes type 1

If no longer controlled properly, diabetes kind 1 can result in some severe headaches consisting of:

- **Hypoglycemia or Low Blood Sugar** - Low blood sugar develops whilst you're taking more than the desired dosage of insulin.
- **Microvascular Complications** - harm to both tiny and huge blood vessels due to out of control blood glucose which may additionally cause eye, kidney or nerve diseases.
- **Macrovascular complications** - Plaque increase inside the arteries main to feasible coronary heart attack or stroke.

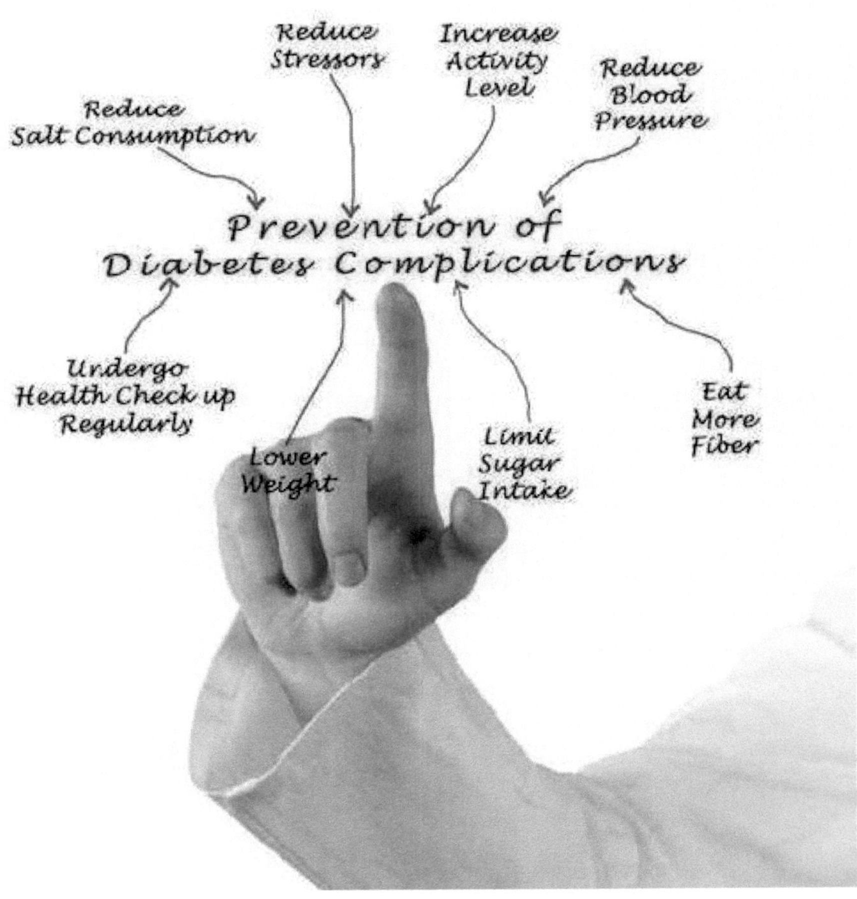

Diabetes mellitus type 2

Diabetes kind 2 is the most not unusual shape of diabetes mellitus inside the global. Insulin resistance via the body is the often determined cause of diabetes type 2. however, there's additionally any other unusual thing which reasons diabetes kind 2, that is, the body clearly does now not produce sufficient insulin.

Insulin is a hormone produced by means of the pancreas that allows the body to apply glucose (a form of sugar located in lots of carbohydrates) for strength. Insulin additionally helps to stability of blood glucose or blood sugar degrees, by preventing it from getting too high **(hyperglycemia)** or too low **(hypoglycemia).**

Symptoms of diabetes type 2

The symptoms of diabetes type 2 include:

- Immoderate urination
- Excessive thirst
- Dry mouth
- Unexpected weight loss
- Fatigue
- Headaches
- Extended starvation
- Blurry imaginative and prescient
- Slow recuperation wounds
- Loss of focus
- Impotency
- Itching skin
- Gradual healing wounds
- Frequent yeast infections (women)

Diagnosis

Diagnosis of diabetes type 2 typically includes one or more blood tests.

- Glycated haemoglobin (A1C) test. This take a look at indicates your blood sugar tiers for the past to three months. This check measures the proportion of haemoglobin — an oxygen-transporting protein in purple blood cells — to which the blood sugar is attached. A excessive percent

of haemoglobin (6.5 % or higher) suggests diabetes.
- Random Blood Sugar check.
- A Fasting Blood Sugar test, and Oral glucose tolerance take a look at.

The complications of diabetes type 2 include:

- Coronary heart palpitations
- Excessive sweating
- Slurred speech
- Whiteness of pores and skin
- Confusion
- Headache
- Tension
- Numbness in fingers, ft, and lips
- Drowsiness

Treatement

Treatments for type 1 and type 2 diabetes

Treatment for type 1 diabetes involves insulin injections or the use of an insulin pump, frequent blood sugar assessments, and carbohydrate counting. treatment of type 2 diabetes in most cases includes lifestyle adjustments, monitoring of your blood sugar, in conjunction with diabetes medicines, insulin or both.

- **Tracking your blood sugar:-** depending to your remedy plan, you may test and record your blood sugar as many as 4 times a day or more regularly if you're taking insulin. cautious tracking is the most effective way to ensure that your blood sugar stage stays within your goal variety. human beings with type 2 diabetes who are not taking insulin generally take a look at their blood sugar a good deal much less often.
- people who obtain insulin therapy additionally may additionally select to monitor their blood sugar levels with a non-stop glucose monitor. despite the factthat this era hasn't yet completely changed the glucose

meter, it could appreciably lessen the quantity of fingerstick necessary to check blood sugar and provide essential information about traits in blood sugar tiers.

- Regardless of cautious management, blood sugar ranges can now and again change unpredictably. With help out of your diabetes remedy crew, you will learn how your blood sugar level changes in response to meals, bodily hobby, medicines, infection, alcohol, strain — and for ladies, fluctuations in hormone degrees.
- Similarly to every day blood sugar monitoring, your medical doctor will probable endorse ordinary A1C testing to degree your common blood sugar degree for the beyond to 3 months.
- Compared with repeated daily blood sugar checks, A1C checking out better indicates how well your diabetes remedy plan is operating overall. An increased A1C level may additionally sign the want for a alternate in your oral medication, insulin routine or meal plan.
- Target A1C purpose may additionally vary depending to age and various different elements, consisting of other clinical conditions you can have. however, for the general public with diabetes, the yank Diabetes association recommends an A1C of underneath 7%. Ask your doctor what your A1C goal is.

- **Insulin**. human beings with type 1 diabetes need insulin therapy to survive. Many humans with type 2 diabetes or gestational diabetes also need insulin therapy.

Many varieties of insulin are available, along with quick-acting (regular insulin), rapid-performing insulin, long-acting insulin and intermediate options. relying for your needs, your physician might also prescribe a mixture of insulin kinds to apply at some point of the day and night time.

Insulin cannot be taken orally to decrease blood sugar due to the fact belly enzymes intrude with insulin's movement. often insulin is injected using a exceptional needle and syringe or an insulin pen — a tool that seems like a large ink pen.

- An **insulin pump** additionally can be an alternative. The pump is a device approximately the size of a small cell cellphone worn on the outside of your body. A tube connects the reservoir of insulin to a catheter it really is inserted underneath the skin of your abdomen.

A tubeless pump that works wirelessly is likewise now available. You application an insulin pump to dispense precise amounts of insulin. it can be adjusted to deliver extra or much less insulin depending on food, hobby stage and blood sugar level.

In September 2016, the food and Drug administration accepted the primary synthetic pancreas for people with kind 1 diabetes who are age 14 and older. A 2d artificial pancreas become approved in December 2019. considering that then, systems had been accredited for youngsters older than 2 years vintage.

- **An synthetic pancreas is likewise called closed-loop insulin delivery.** The implanted tool hyperlinks a continuous glucose screen, which checks blood sugar tiers every 5 mins, to an insulin pump. The device routinely offers the correct quantity of insulin while the reveal shows it is needed.

Oral or different medicinal drugs. from time to time other oral or injected medications are prescribed as nicely. a few diabetes medicines stimulate your pancreas to provide and launch extra insulin. Others inhibit the manufacturing and release of glucose from your liver, which means you need less insulin to transport sugar into your cells.
nonetheless others block the movement of belly or intestinal enzymes that destroy down carbohydrates or make your tissues greater touchy to insulin. Metformin (Glumetza, Fortamet, others) is normally the primary medicinal drug prescribed for type 2 diabetes.
another magnificence of medicine referred to as SGLT2 inhibitors can be used. They paintings through stopping the kidneys from reabsorbing sugar into the blood. as a substitute, the sugar is excreted within the urine.

- **Transplantation.** In a few people who have type 1 diabetes, a pancreas transplant can be an option. Islet transplants are being studied as nicely. With a a hit pancreas transplant, you will no longer want insulin remedy.

but transplants are not constantly a success — and these methods pose serious risks. You need an entire life of immune-suppressing drugs to save you organ rejection. these capsules may have extreme side effects, that is why transplants are normally reserved for human beings whose diabetes can not be controlled or folks who additionally want a kidney transplant.

- **Bariatric surgical procedure.** even though it is not specially taken into consideration a treatment for type 2 diabetes, human beings with type 2 diabetes who're obese and have a frame mass index better than 35 may gain from this type of surgery. humans who've gone through gastric bypass have seen big improvements in their blood sugar tiers. however, this technique's long-term dangers and benefits for kind 2 diabetes are not yet recognised.

-

OGTT: Indications, Procedure, Interpretation and t ypes of GTT curve

The OGTT evaluates how the body manages glucose after a meal. Glucose is a type of sugar produced while the frame breaks down carbohydrates fed on in meals. a number of the glucose might be used for power; the rest may be saved for destiny use.

the quantity of glucose in your blood is controlled with the aid of the hormones insulin and glucagon. if body have an excessive amount of, the pancreas secretes insulin to assist cells soak up and keep glucose. if body have too little, the pancreas secretes glucagon in order that saved glucose can be launched returned into the bloodstream.

beneath normal instances, the frame can be able to keep the appropriate balance of blood glucose. however, if any parts of the gadget are impaired, glucose can unexpectedly collect, leading to excessive blood sugar (hyperglycemia) and diabetes.

lack of insulin or insulin resistance causes better than everyday stages of glucose inside the blood.

The OGTT is a rather sensitive test that can discover imbalances that different checks leave out. The country wide Institute of Diabetes and Digestive and Kidney sicknesses (NIDDK) recommends the OGTT for the subsequent purposes:2

- Screening and diagnosis of prediabetes or impaired glucose tolerance (IGT)
- Screening and prognosis of type 2 diabetes
- Screening and prognosis of gestational diabetes

Amongst its different uses, the OGTT may be ordered to diagnose reactive hypoglycemia (wherein blood sugar drops after ingesting), acromegaly (an overactive pituitary gland), beta cellular disorder (in which insulin isn't being secreted), and rare problems affecting carbohydrate metabolism (which includes hereditary fructose intolerance).

Types

The OGTT process can vary significantly based totally at the desires of the check. The concentration of the oral glucose can vary as can the timing and number of blood attracts required. There are even versions wherein a low-carbohydrate food regimen may be prescribed.

There are preferred versions used for screening and diagnostic purposes:

- **A two-hour OGTT**, produced from blood attracts, is used to diagnose diabetes/prediabetes in non-pregnant adults and children.
- **A 3-hour OGTT**, produced from four blood draws, is used to display gestational diabetes.

Pregnancy Recommendations

The american college of Obstetricians and Gynecologists (ACOG) recommends the habitual screening for gestational diabetes in all pregnant women among 24 and 28 weeks of gestation.

With that being stated, rather than proceeding at once to a 3-hour OGTT, healthcare companies will frequently suggest a one-hour glucose venture first, which does not require fasting. the one-hour glucose task can be ordered before 24 weeks if you are obese, have a circle of relatives records of diabetes, are identified with polycystic ovary syndrome (PCOS), or have experienced gestational diabetes within the beyond.4 If the effects of the test are odd—with blood glucose values same to or more than 140 milligrams consistent with deciliter (mg/dL)—you will be stepped as much as the total, three-hour OGTT. a few healthcare companies set the brink as low as 130 mg/dL.

Advantages and Disadvantages

The OGTT is far more sensitive than the fasting plasma glucose take a look at (FPG) and is frequently ordered when diabetes is suspected however the FPG returns a regular result.5 Its ability to detect early impairment way that human beings with prediabetes can regularly deal with their situation with weight-reduction plan and exercising as opposed to drugs.

The OGTT is likewise the most effective test that can definitively diagnose IGT.

despite those blessings, the OGTT has its obstacles:

- The OGTT is a time-eating take a look at, requiring significant pre-test fasting and a prolonged trying out and ready duration.
- The test outcomes can be influenced with the aid of pressure, infection, or medicinal drugs.
- Blood is less solid after collection, that means that the effects can every so often be skewed as a result of improper dealing with or garage of the sample.
- In terms of accuracy, the OGTT has a sensitivity (the proportion of correct high-quality take a look at effects) of between eighty one percent and 93 percentage. this is some distance higher than the FGP, which has a sensitivity of between forty five percent and 54 percentage.

Risks and Contraindications

The OGTT is a safe and minimally invasive check that requires two to four blood draws.

contamination is unusual but may also occur.

However, some might also have a reaction to the oral glucose answer, most usually nausea or vomiting. If vomiting occurs at some stage in checking out, the take a look at won't be completed.

An OGTT must no longer be finished if :

- Already have a confirmed diabetes prognosis
- Have an allergic reaction to sugar or dextrose
- Are convalescing from surgical procedure, trauma, or contamination
- Are underneath excessive psychological pressure

- Have ever skilled hypokalemic paralysis

HbA1c

Hemoglobin A1c (HbA1c) test

A hemoglobin A1c (HbA1c) test measures the quantity of blood sugar (glucose) connected to hemoglobin. Hemoglobin is the a part of your crimson blood cells that includes oxygen from your lungs to the relaxation of your frame. An HbA1c test indicates what the average quantity of glucose connected to hemoglobin has been during the last three months.

In case body HbA1c stages are excessive, it is able to be a sign of diabetes, a chronic circumstance that can purpose critical health issues, along with coronary heart sickness, kidney disorder, and nerve damage.

Different names: HbA1c, A1c, glycohemoglobin, glycated hemoglobin, glycosylated hemoglobin

Uses

An HbA1c test can be used to check for diabetes or prediabetes in adults. Prediabetes means your blood sugar stages display you are at hazard forgetting diabetes.

Results means

HbA1c results are given in percentages. Typical results are below.

- **Normal**: HbA1c below 5.7%
- **Prediabetes:** HbA1c between 5.7% and 6.4%
- **Diabetes:** HbA1c of 6.5% or higher

Hypoglycemia-definition & causes

Hypoglycemia is a condition wherein your blood sugar (glucose) level is lower than ordinary. Glucose is your body's primary energy supply.

Hypoglycemia is often related to diabetes remedy. however other tablets and an expansion of conditions — many uncommon — can reason low blood sugar in folks that don't have diabetes

Hypoglycemia wishes instant treatment when blood sugar stages are low. for many humans, a fasting blood sugar of 70 milligrams consistent with deciliter (mg/dL), or 39 millimoles consistent with liter (mmol/L), or beneath should serve as an alert for hypoglycemia. but your numbers might be extraordinary.

Treatment includes fast getting your blood sugar again to normal either with excessive-sugar ingredients or liquids or with medicinal drugs. long-term remedy requires figuring out and treating the motive of hypoglycemia.

Causes

Hypoglycemia takes place while your blood sugar (glucose) level falls too low. There are several reasons why this may occur; the maximum common is impact of drugs used to deal with diabetes.

Blood sugar regulation

Body breaks down carbohydrates from ingredients — such as bread, rice, pasta, veggies, fruit and milk products — into diverse sugar molecules, which includes glucose.

Glucose, the primary electricity supply on your frame, enters the cells of maximum of your tissues with the assist of insulin — a hormone secreted via your pancreas. Insulin allows the glucose to go into the cells and offer the fuel your cells need. greater glucose is stored for your liver and muscular tissues within the form of glycogen.

If you have not eaten for numerous hours and your blood sugar stage drops, every other hormone out of your pancreas signals your liver to interrupt down the stored glycogen and launch glucose into your bloodstream. This maintains your blood sugar inside a normal variety until you consume once more.

Your body additionally has the potential to make glucose. This system takes place especially to your liver, however additionally on your kidneys.

Possible causes, with diabetes

when you have diabetes, you might not make sufficient insulin (type 1 diabetes) otherwise you is probably much less conscious of it (type 2 diabetes). As a end result, glucose has a tendency to build up inside the bloodstream and might attain dangerously high ranges. To correct this problem, you may take insulin or other pills to decrease blood sugar ranges.

However an excessive amount of insulin or different diabetes medicinal drugs may also motive your blood sugar level to drop too low, causing hypoglycemia. Hypoglycemia can also arise in case you eat much less than regular after taking diabetes medicinal drug, or if you exercise greater than you generally do.

Possible causes, without diabetes

Hypoglycemia in people without diabetes is much less common. Causes can include the following:

- **Medications.** Taking someone else's oral diabetes medication accidentally is a possible cause of hypoglycemia. Other medications can cause hypoglycemia, especially in children or in people with kidney failure. One example is quinine (Qualaquin), used to treat malaria.
- **Excessive alcohol drinking.** Drinking heavily without eating can block your liver from releasing stored glucose into your bloodstream, causing hypoglycemia.
- **Some critical illnesses.** Severe liver illnesses such as severe hepatitis or cirrhosis can cause hypoglycemia. Kidney disorders, which can keep your body from properly excreting medications, can affect glucose levels due to a build-up of those medications.

Long-term hunger, as can occur inside the eating disorder anorexia nervosa, can result in too little of substances your frame wishes to create glucose.

- **Insulin overproduction**. a rare tumor of the pancreas (insulinoma) can motive you to supply an excessive amount of insulin, ensuing in hypoglycemia. other tumours also can bring about an excessive amount of manufacturing of insulin-like substances. enlargement of cells of the pancreas that produce insulin can result in immoderate insulin launch, causing hypoglycemia.
- **Hormone deficiencies.** positive adrenal gland and pituitary tumor disorders can bring about a deficiency of key hormones that regulate glucose manufacturing. children can have hypoglycemia if they have too little increase hormone.

CHAPTER II

Lipids

Lipids

- Fatty acids: Definition, classification
- Definition & Clinical significance of MUFA & PUFA, Essential fatty acids, Trans fatty acids
- Digestion, absorption & metabolism of lipids & related disorders
- Compounds formed from cholesterol
- Ketone bodies (name, types & significance only)
- Lipoproteins – types & functions (metabolism not required)
- Lipid profile
- Atherosclerosis (in brief)

Fatty acid

Fatty acids (FAs) are a class of lipids comprising carbon, hydrogen, and oxygen, arranged as the linear structure of a flexible carbon chain, usually with an equal number of atoms, with a carboxyl group at the end.
Acidic fatty acids of 2 to 30 carbon or more are possible, but the most common and essential contain between 12 and 22 carbon atoms and are found in most animal and plant fats.
They are rarely free in nature and are the main components:

- Triglycerides (or triglycerides).
- Diacylglycerols.
- Monoacylglycerols (the last two families of compounds are often added to processed foods).
- Cell membrane phospholipids.
- Sterol esters.

Classification

Depending on their carbon / non-saturation level, they can be divided into three classes:

- saturated fatty acids (SFAs), if no double bond is present;
- monounsaturated fatty acids (MUFAs), if there is one double bond;
- polyunsaturated fatty acids (PUFAs), if there are two or more double bonds.

In addition on the basis of the absence / presence of double / triple bonds can be divided into two broad classes:

- Saturated FAs, if there are no double bonds in the carbon chain;
- Unsaturated FA, if there is one or more bonds doubled in a carbon chain.

Definition & Clinical significance of MUFA & PUFA, Essential fatty acids, Trans fatty acids

1. Monounsaturated fatty acids (MUFA)

These are healthy fat molecules with double bond fatty chains and the remaining carbon atoms combined. Vegetable oils rich in MUFA are not liquid at room temperature and are almost semisolid or solid when cold. The abundant natural food sources in MUFA are dairy products, nuts, seeds, olives and avocados and are a major part of the Mediterranean diet. Sunflower oil contains 85% MUFA, olive oil 75% and canola oil 58%. Some of the other good sources of MUFA are almonds, corn, sesame seeds, nuts, grape seeds, safflower and wheat grains.

2. Polyunsaturated Fatty Acids (PUFA)

Polyunsaturated fatty acids (PUFA) are healthy lipid molecules with two or more carbon-carbon double bonds. PUFA-rich oils are not liquid at room temperature, the viscosity and temperature of the melting point rise in reverse to become a double bond. Good sources for PUFA are walnut, sunflower seeds, flax seeds and poppy seeds.

PUFA is two types of omega 3 fatty acids and omega 6 fatty acids. Omega 3 fatty acids are 3 types of linoleic acid, Eicosapentaenoic Acid and Docosahexaenoic Acid and are abundant in fish and other vegetable sources are chia seeds, hemp seeds and flax seeds.

Rich sources of Omega-6 Fatty Acids palm oil, soybeans, rapeseed, and sunflower.

Foods high in omega-6 fatty acids eggs, whole grains, nuts, pumpkin seeds, pine nuts, walnuts. However, the main food sources for EPA and

DHA are fish oil and krill oil.

Health Benefits Of MUFA And PUFA

Omega 3 fatty acids have powerful anti-inflammatory properties that reduce the risk of heart disease, Alzheimer's, promote vision and improve brain health.

Choose MUFA and PUFA-rich fats instead of saturated fats and other unhealthy fats as they can reduce the risk of heart disease.

MUFA is good for improving insulin levels and keeps blood sugar under control, thus avoiding conditions of hyperglycemia, hypoglycemia and prediabetes symptoms.

Evidence has shown that regular use of MUFA lowers bad cholesterol and improves good cholesterol levels.

Omega 3 fatty acids rich in PUFA promote mood and reduce stress and anxiety.

Omega 3 fatty acids promote normal baby growth.

Diet of MUFA and PUFA as a supplement helps maintain cells and nerves and aids digestion.

The key is balance as eating too much fat can increase the risk of chronic diseases.

Essential Fatty Acids

Essential oils, or EFAs, are fatty acids that should be consumed by humans and other animals because they are needed by the body for good health but cannot be synthesized. The fatty acids needed for biological processes are called "essential fatty acids" but do not include fats that only act as fuel. In the sense of distilled essence, essential fatty acids should not be confused with essential oils, "essential" Here is an example of Two Essential Fatty AcidsLinoleic acid (omega-6 fatty acid) and alpha-linolenic acid. composed of many types (omega-3 fatty acids). However, in cellular processes and the development of other omega-3 and omega-6 essential fatty acids, certain fatty acids are needed. Therefore, they are called fatty acids because they need to be taken with food. Omega-6 and omega-3 fatty acids found in linoleic acid and alpha-linolenic acid, respectively, are conditionally required by most mammals; they are produced from their fatty acids in the body, but not always at sufficient levels to maintain health or high growth.

Trans fat, or trans-fatty acids

These are unsaturated fatty acids from natural or industrial sources. Natural fat is derived from grazing animals (cattle and sheep). Industrial trans fats are manufactured by an industrial process that adds hydrogen to vegetable oils and converts liquids into solids, resulting in partially "hydrogenated" oils (PHO).

Digestion, absorption & metabolism of lipids & related disorders

Digestion and Absorption of Lipids

Lipids are large molecules and usually do not dissolve in water. Like carbohydrates and proteins, lipids are broken down into smaller portions for absorption. Since many of our digestive enzymes are based on water, how does the body break down fats and make them available for a variety of functions to the human body.

From the Mouth to the Stomach

The first step in digesting triglycerides and phospholipids begins in the mouth as the lipids interact with saliva. Next, the body's digestive action combined with the action of emulsifiers enables digestive enzymes to perform their functions. The enzyme lingual lipase, along with a small amount of phospholipid as an emulsifier, initiates the digestive process. These actions make fat more easily accessible to digestive enzymes. As a result, the oil becomes smaller droplets and separated from the water particles.

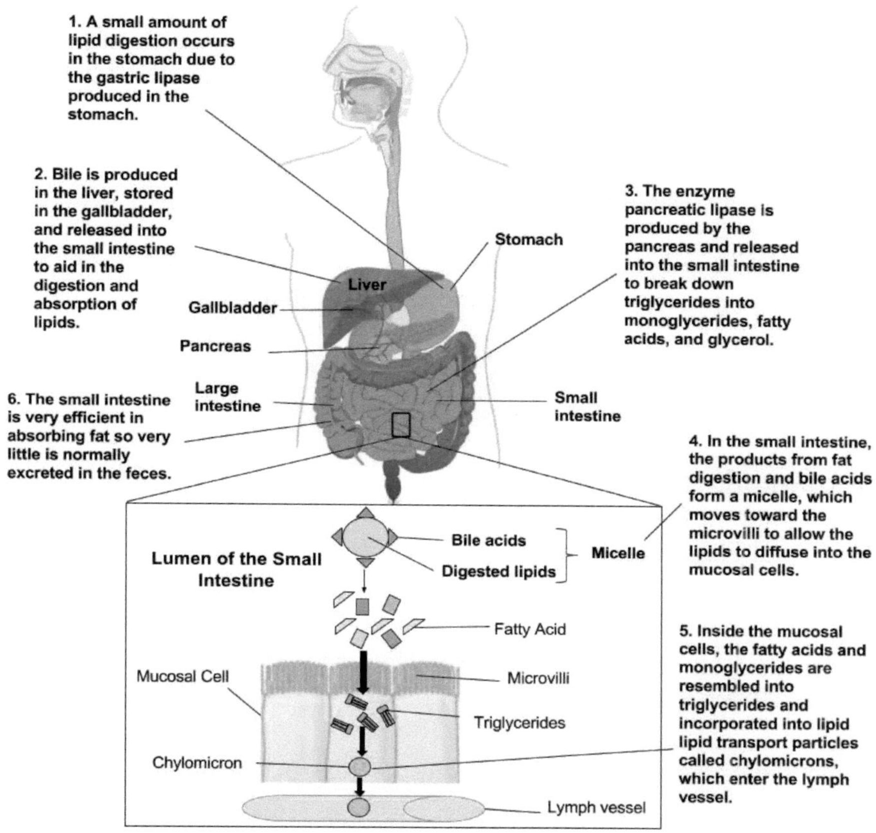

Lipid Digestion and Absorption

In the stomach, gastric lipase begins to break down triglycerides into diglycerides and fatty acids. Within two to four hours after eating a meal, about 30 percent of triglycerides are converted into diglycerides and fatty acids. Stomach digestion and constipation help dissolve fat cells, while the diglycerides found in this process act as additional emulsifiers. Yet, even in the midst of all this activity, there is very little fat in the stomach.

Disorders

- Disorders of lipid metabolism, such as Gaucher's disease and Tay-Sachs' disease, involve lipids. Lipids are fats or substances such as fats. They include fats, fatty acids, waxes, and cholesterol. If you have one of these disorders, you may not have enough enzymes to break down lipids. Or the enzymes may not work properly and your body will not be able to convert fat into energy. They cause a dangerous amount of lipids to form in your body. Over time, that can damage your cells and tissues, especially your brain, the nervous system, the liver, spleen, and bone marrow. Many of these diseases can be very serious, or sometimes fatal.

- These diseases are inherited. Newborn babies are tested for some of them, using a blood test. If there is a family history of one of these problems, parents can get a genetic test to determine if they have a genetic predisposition. A genetic test may reveal whether an embryo is infected or not.

Compounds formed from cholesterol

Many compounds are derived from cholesterol.

BILE SALTS

- Bile salt promotes the absorption and absorption of dietary fats. Sodium glycocholate is an important salt of bile.

STEROID HORMONES

Progestogens

- Progesterone is responsible for preparing the body for pregnancy and storing it until birth.

Glucocorticoids

- Cortisol plays an important role in glucose metabolism.

Mineralocorticoids

- Aldosterone increases blood pressure and blood pressure by increasing Na^+ re-absorption and K^+ and H^+ kidney excretion.

Androgens

- Testosterone is responsible for the development and maintenance of secondary male sexual characteristics.

Estrogens

- Estrogens are involved in the development and maintenance of female reproductive organs.

VITAMIN D

- Vitamin D is one of the cholesterol-releasing groups in the body responsible for improving intestinal absorption of calcium, iron, magnesium, phosphate, and zinc.

Ketone bodies (name, types & significance)

Ketone Bodies

Ketone bodies, or ketones, are just substances that the liver produces during gluconeogenesis, a process that produces glucose during periods of fasting and starvation. There are three ketone bodies produced by the liver. They are acetoacetate, beta-hydroxybutyrate, and acetone. These compounds are used in healthy people to provide energy to the body's cells when glucose is low or absent in the diet.

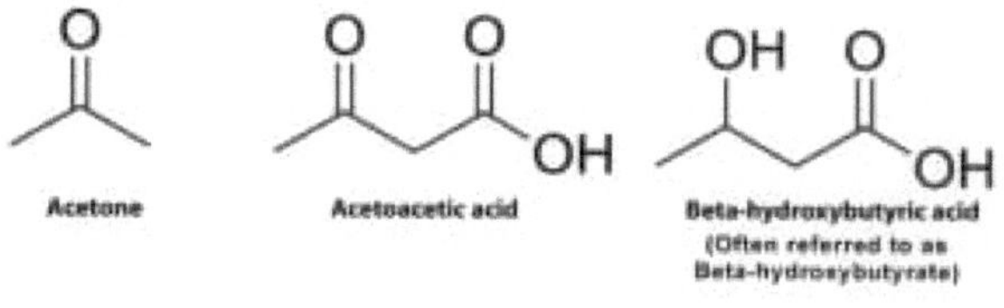

Above are the three ketone bodies. Acetone (left), acetoacetate (middle), beta-hydroxybutyrate (right).

significance

- **Ketone Bodies in Diabetes**

Diabetes is a condition in which the body cannot or does not produce insulin, an important molecule in the glucose cycle. Insulin shows the body's cells to absorb glucose from the blood and use it for energy. For those with diabetes, this signal is inaccessible and without synthetic insulin, glucose will remain trapped in the bloodstream. Without glucose in the cells, the body begins to absorb fatty acids in the blood, to provide energy.

Lack of glucose also causes the liver to start producing glucose. As this happens, ketone bodies are released, just like in a normal person. However, the person with diabetes has an additional problem. Ketone bodies can be used for energy, but only if there are suitable coordinates. This is usually due to the breakdown of glucose. However, in a person with diabetes, too little glucose has been reduced. This means that even ketone bodies cannot be used for energy. Therefore, they begin to build quickly.

This causes sudden and severe ketoacidosis. Diabetes is usually found in the smell of acetone or fruit in the human soul and in the urine filled with acetone. These symptoms indicate severe ketoacidosis and can be dangerous to health. Fortunately, the insulin level will allow for lower blood sugar levels, the necessary content will be created from the breakdown of glucose, and ketone bodies will be released from the system in a short time.

Researchers are testing the Keto Diet as a way to reduce diabetes - although they warn that any diabetics on the Keto diet should be under medical supervision because diet can lead to significant changes in blood glucose levels that can be harmful.

- **Ketone Bodies in Dieting and Starvation**

Interestingly, some recent diets have been linked to ketoacidosis in humans. These foods focus on low carbohydrates and high protein. Because carbohydrates are complex types of sugars, eliminating them from the diet effectively removes glucose from the diet. This works for a while because the body needs to get the energy it needs from fat. However, food actually mimics your body in starvation mode.

In addition to glucose in the blood, cells in the body also need to survive fatty acids, which are found in stored triglycerides. The brain cannot survive without these fatty acids, and the liver must undergo gluconeogenesis to produce glucose in the brain. While doing this, it also produces ketone bodies. In a short time, the body is able to absorb its energy in this way. However, as glucose levels drop and fall, so do middlemen needed to use ketone bodies as energy. Eventually, more ketone bodies will be formed than can be used, and they begin to build up. They are excreted by the kidneys, but the kidneys can remove most of the time.

Even if a person still eats these foods, a complete lack of carbohydrates makes it very difficult for the body to adapt to the diet, and acidosis begins to occur. Like a person with diabetes, the level of acetone in the urine will increase and the air may smell sweet or as acetone.

The creators of these diets often refer to this as a "normal eating disorder", but ketoacidosis is rare in healthy people and forcing your body into that condition can be dangerous. Above are some of the listed symptoms of acidosis. In addition, it has been found that blood acidosis can lead to low levels of calcium in the diet and into the bones. This means that you not only starve yourself, but also weaken your bones.

Lipoproteins – types & functions

Cholesterol and triglycerides are fatty molecules. Because of their fat-like properties, they cannot circulate easily in the blood. To keep cholesterol and triglycerides in the bloodstream, they are often loaded with proteins that cause cholesterol and triglycerides to dissolve more in the blood. This lipid and protein structure is called lipoprotein.

Types and Functions

There are five different types of lipoproteins in the blood, and they are usually classified according to their density. The main types of lipoproteins analyzed by the lipid panel include low-density lipoproteins (VLDS), low-density lipoproteins (LDL), and high-density lipoproteins (HDL).

- **Very Low-Density Lipoproteins (VLDL)**

These lipoproteins contain mainly triglycerides, other cholesterol molecules, and small amounts of protein. In this case, VLDL is less concentrated than most lipoproteins due to its high lipid structure.

VLDL is produced in the liver and is responsible for delivering triglycerides to cells in the body, which are essential for cellular processes. As triglycerides are sent to cells, VLDL is made up of less fat and more protein, leaving cholesterol in the molecule. As this process progresses,

VLDL will eventually become an LDL molecule.

- **Low-Density Lipoproteins (LDL)**

LDL contains more cholesterol than triglycerides and proteins. Because it contains less lipid and more protein compared to VLDL, its density is greater. LDL is responsible for transporting cholesterol to the cells it needs.

High LDL levels are associated with an increased risk of cardiovascular disease. Certain types of LDL — particularly small, high-density LDL (sdLDL) (sdLDL) and oxidized LDL (oxLDL) — have been linked to the development of atherosclerosis by placing fat on the walls of blood vessels in the body.

Because high levels of LDL are associated with the development of heart disease, LDL is also known as "bad" cholesterol.

- **High-Density Lipoprotein (HDL)**

Compared to LDL, HDL contains less cholesterol and more protein, making these lipoproteins more dense. HDL is produced in the liver and intestines. It is responsible for transporting cholesterol from the cells back to the liver. Because of this, HDL is also considered "good" cholesterol.

- **Other Lipoproteins**

There are other lipoproteins that are also involved in transporting fat to cells, but they are rarely measured by the normal lipid panel. These include:

Cylomicrons are slightly dense in all lipoproteins. These molecules are composed mainly of triglycerides and a small amount of protein. Cylomicrons are responsible for transporting lipids from the intestinal tract to cells in the body.

Intermediate density lipoproteins (IDL) are slightly thicker than LDL molecules but thicker than VLDL particles. As triglycerides in VLDL are broken down by the cells they need, the particles become thicker due to changes in lipid and protein balance.

This causes VLDL to be converted to IDL. As triglycerides and cholesterol are introduced into more cells in the body, IDL will gradually be converted to LDL.

Lipid profile

Lipid Profile Testing is actually a series of tests performed together to check the amount of cholesterol (and its subtypes) in the blood. Lipid profile test results can help us understand, measure, monitor, diagnose and prevent many medical conditions, some of which can be fatal. It can also help us to identify and measure the continuity or success of alternative therapies, treatments and changes that may occur at the same time.

Lipids Definition

Lipids in fat cells (as well as fatty substances) circulate in the bloodstream and are present in body tissues. Lipids are an important part of the body, and they provide energy for our daily activities. In addition, they are known to help ensure the proper functioning of the nervous system which includes signal transmission and brain development (and nerves). Disorders, imbalances or irregularities in lipid formation can lead to a number of diseases - some of which are naturally life-threatening - heart attack, stroke, or peripheral artery disease.

Importantence

Anyone over the age of 20 should undergo a Lipid Profile Test once a year. Men over the age of 45 and women over the age of 50 should do it twice a year, or as prescribed by their doctor. For those who already have a heart condition or heart disease, or who have studied abnormalities at the first stage of the Lipid Profile Test, they should go for regular check-ups.

Lipid Profile tests are performed to detect cholesterol levels (including 'bad cholesterol') and triglycerides in the body and thus to measure the risk levels of various cardiovascular diseases and blood cells.

A Lipid Profile Test may also be prescribed for individuals who:

- Are you overweight or obese
- Have an existing heart disease
- They suffer from diabetes or are at risk of developing a condition known as prediabetes
- Live a sedentary lifestyle
- They tend to eat unhealthy and unhealthy foods
- She is suffering from chronic hypertension
- Make a habit of smoking or drinking
- Have a family history of premature heart disease or dyslipidemia (abnormal cholesterol levels and lipid levels in the body)

Atherosclerosis

Arteriosclerosis occurs when the blood vessels that carry oxygen and nutrients from your heart to your entire body (blood vessels) become thicker and stronger - sometimes blocking the flow of blood to your organs and muscles. Healthy arteries are flexible and flexible, but over time, the walls in your arteries may become stiff, a condition commonly called arterial stiffness.

Atherosclerosis is a specific type of arteriosclerosis.

Atherosclerosis is the build-up of fats, cholesterol, and other substances in and on the walls of arteries. This buildup is called plaque. Plaque can narrow the arteries and block blood flow. Plaque can also rupture and form blood clots.

Atherosclerosis is often considered a disease of the heart, but it can affect any artery in the body. Atherosclerosis can be treated. A healthy lifestyle can help prevent hardening of the arteries.

Symptoms

Mild atherosclerosis usually doesn't have any symptoms.

You usually won't have atherosclerosis symptoms until an artery is so narrowed or clogged that it can't supply enough blood to your organs and tissues. Sometimes a blood clot completely blocks blood flow, or even breaks apart and can trigger a heart attack or stroke.

Symptoms of moderate to severe atherosclerosis depend on which arteries are affected.

For example:

If you have atherosclerosis in your heart arteries, you may have symptoms, such as chest pain or pressure (angina).

If you have atherosclerosis in the arteries leading to your brain, you may have signs and symptoms such as sudden numbness or weakness in your arms or legs, difficulty speaking or slurred speech, temporary loss of vision in one eye, or drooping muscles in your face. These signal a transient ischemic attack (TIA), which, if left untreated, may progress to a stroke.

If you have atherosclerosis in the arteries in your arms and legs, you may have signs or symptoms of peripheral artery disease, such as leg pain when walking (claudication) or decreased blood pressure in an affected limb.

If you have atherosclerosis in the arteries leading to your kidneys, you develop high blood pressure or kidney failure.

Mild atherosclerosis usually doesn't have any signs and symptoms.

You normally might not have atherosclerosis signs until an artery is so narrowed or clogged that it can not supply sufficient blood to your organs and tissues. on occasion a blood clot absolutely blocks blood glide, or maybe breaks apart and might trigger a heart attack or stroke.

symptoms of moderate to intense atherosclerosis depend on which arteries are affected.

As an instance:

If you have atherosclerosis on your heart arteries, you may have signs, which include chest ache or stress (angina).

If you have atherosclerosis inside the arteries leading to your brain, you could have signs and symptoms and symptoms inclusive of surprising numbness or weak spot in your arms or legs, difficulty speaking or slurred speech, brief lack of vision in one eye, or drooping muscle tissue for your face. those signal a brief ischemic attack (TIA), which, if left untreated, may also progress to a stroke.

If you have atherosclerosis inside the arteries for your arms and legs, you may have signs and symptoms or signs and symptoms of peripheral artery disease, together with leg ache when strolling (claudication) or decreased blood pressure in an affected limb.

If you have atherosclerosis inside the arteries main to your kidneys, you increase excessive blood stress or kidney failure.

Causes

Atherosclerosis is a slow, modern disease that may start as early as youth. although the precise purpose is unknown, atherosclerosis may begin with damage or injury to the inner layer of an artery. The damage may be due to:

- High blood strain.
- High cholesterol.
- Excessive triglycerides, a kind of fat (lipid) for your blood.

- Smoking and different sources of tobacco.
- Insulin resistance, weight problems or diabetes.
- Irritation from an unknown reason or from diseases including arthritis, lupus, psoriasis or inflammatory bowel ailment.

Risk factors

Hardening of the arteries takes place over time. besides growing old, factors that may boom your chance of atherosclerosis include:

1. High blood pressure
2. Excessive cholesterol
3. Excessive levels of C-reactive protein (CRP), a marker of inflammation
4. Diabetes
5. Weight problems
6. Sleep apnea
7. Smoking and other tobacco use
8. A own family history of early heart disease
9. Loss of exercise
10. An bad food plan

Complications

The complicationsd of atherosclerosis depend on which arteries are blocked. for instance:

- **Coronary artery ailment**. when atherosclerosis narrows the arteries near your heart, you could develop coronary artery ailment, which could motive chest pain (angina), a heart attack or coronary heart failure.Carotid artery ailment. when atherosclerosis narrows the arteries close to your brain, you may expand carotid artery ailment, that could purpose a temporary ischemic attack (TIA) or stroke.
- **Peripheral artery disease.** while atherosclerosis narrows the arteries to your fingers or legs, you may develop movement problems on your arms and legs called peripheral artery ailment. this can make you much less touchy to warmness and bloodless, increasing your threat of burns or frostbite. In uncommon instances, terrible flow in your hands or legs can purpose tissue demise (gangrene).
- **Aneurysms.** Atherosclerosis can also purpose aneurysms, a critical worry which can occur anywhere for your frame. An aneurysm is a bulge

in the wall of your artery.

Most people with aneurysms don't have any symptoms. pain and throbbing within the place of an aneurysm might also occur and is a scientific emergency.

If an aneurysm bursts, you could face life-threatening internal bleeding. although this is often a unexpected, catastrophic occasion, a slow leak is viable. If a blood clot within an aneurysm dislodges, it may block an artery at a few remote point.

Chronic kidney disorder. Atherosclerosis can reason the arteries main to your kidneys to slender, stopping oxygenated blood from attaining them. over time, this will have an effect on your kidney feature, maintaining waste from exiting your frame.

Prevention

The identical healthy way lifestyle modification recommended to treat atherosclerosis additionally assist prevent it. Those encompass:

1. Quitting smoking
2. Ingesting wholesome meals
3. Exercising often
4. Keeping a healthful weight
5. Checking and preserving a wholesome blood pressure
6. Checking and preserving healthful cholesterol and blood sugar stages.

CHAPTER III

Proteins

Proteins

- Classification of amino acids based on nutrition,metabolic rate with examples
- Digestion, absorption & metabolism of protein & related disorders
- Biologically important compounds synthesized from various amino acids (only names)
- In born errors of amino acid metabolism – only aromatic amino acids (in brief)
- Plasma protein – types, function & normal values
- Causes of proteinuria, hypoproteinemia, hyper-gamma globinemia
- Principle of electrophoresis, normal & abnormal
- electrophoretic patterns (in brief)

Classification of amino acids based on nutrition

Amino Acids

Proteins are complicated macromolecules made up of amino acids which are located in all residing cells. Amino acids, in other words, are the constructing blocks of proteins. There are around 500 obviously taking place amino acids that we're aware about.

Structure of Amino Acids

Amino acids are the fundamental additives of proteins. Natural materials containing both amino and carboxylic agencies are known as amino acids.

Any carbon atom aside from that of the carboxyl (–COOH) group may be related to the amino group (–NH2).

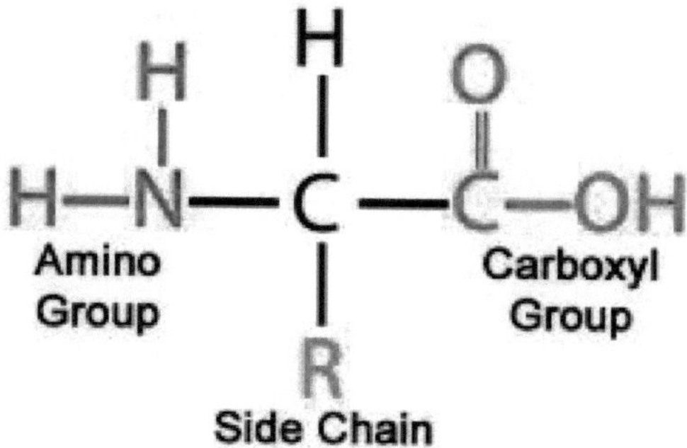

Properties of Amino Acids

- They may be crystalline, colourless compounds.
- Their melting factor is clearly high.
- The nature of the side chain affects the solubility in water.
- They're amphoteric, which means they react with acids and bases.
- Except for glycine, all have asymmetric carbon, which reasons aircraft polarised light to rotate. Optical activity is the name for this feature.

Classification of Amino Acids

Type based totally at the Requirement of the body:

Non-eseential amino acids: those amino acids are produced by the body and do now not want to be fed on. Out of the twenty amino acids, ten are non-important. Glycine, alanine, serine, cysteine, glutamine, tyrosine, proline, aspartic acid, asparagine, and glutamic acid are amino acid.

Essential Amino Acids: these amino acids are not synthesized with the aid of the frame and have to be obtained from food. Out of the twenty amino acids, ten are non-essential. Valine, leucine, isoleucine, arginine, lysine, threonine, phenylalanine, tryptophan, and histidine are the amino acids that make up the human body. those important amino acids are necessary for our our bodies to develop, and a loss of them in our diet can result in issues like kwashiorkor.

Metabolism of Amino Acids

The amino acids undergo sure common reactions like transamination observed via deamination for the liberation of ammonia. The amino group of the amino acids is applied for the formation of urea that is an excretory give up made of protein metabolism.

The carbon skeleton of the amino acids is first transformed to keto acids (by way of transamination) which meet one or greater of the following fates:

1. utilized to generate electricity.

2. Used for the synthesis of glucose.

3. Diverted for the formation of fat or ketone our bodies.

4. Invoved inside the production of non-vital amino acids.

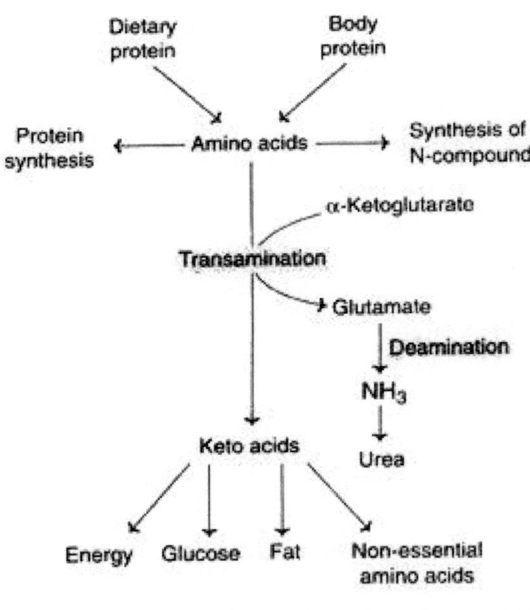

An overview of amino acid metabolism

Transamination:

The transfer of an amino (~NH2) group from an amino acid to a keto acid is referred to as transamination . This system entails the inter-conversion of a pair of amino acids and a pair of keto acids, catalysed through a set of enzymes referred to as transaminases (recently, aminotransferases).

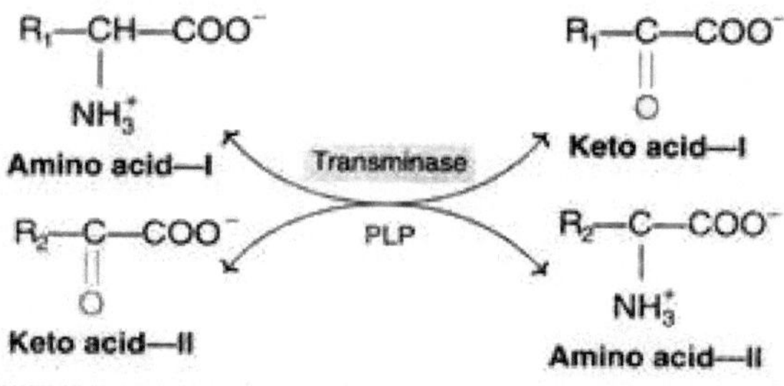

transmission reaction

The salient features of transamination are:

The salient functions of transamination are:

1. All transaminases require pyridoxal phosphate (PLP), a coenzyme derived from nutrition B6.

2. there's no loose NH3 liberated; handiest the transfer of amino institution takes place.

3. Transamination is reversible.

4. It involves each catabolism (degradation) and anabolism (synthesis) of amino acids. Transamination is in the long run liable for the synthesis of non-critical amino acids.

5. Transamination diverts the excess amino acids toward energy generation.

6. The amino acids go through transamination to in the end concentrate

nitrogen in glutamate. Clutamate is the only amino acid that undergoes oxidative deamination to a huge volume to disencumber loose N3 for urea synthesis.

7. All amino acids except lysine, threonine, proline and hydroxyproline participate in transamination .

Deamination:

The removal of amino group from the amino acids as NH3 is deamination. It results within the liberation of ammonia for urea synthesis. Deamination may be both oxidative or non- oxidative.

Urea Cycle:

Urea is the quit product of protein metabolism (amino acid metabolism). The nitrogen of amino acids converted to ammonia is toxic to the body . it's miles converted to urea and detoxified. As such, urea accounts for 80-90% of the nitrogen containing materials excreted in urine.

Urea is synthesized in liver and transported to kidneys for excretion in urine. Urea cycle is the primary metabolic cycle that turned into elucidated via Hans Krebs and Kurt Henseleit (1932), consequently it's far referred to as Krebs-Henseleit cycle. The character reactions, however, had been described in extra detail afterward with the aid of Ratner and Cohen.

Urea has amino (—NH2) agencies, one derived from NH3 and the alternative from aspartate. Carbon atom is furnished with the aid of CO2. Urea synthesis is a 5-step cyclic procedure, with five wonderful enzymes. the primary two enzymes are present in mitochondria at the same time as the relaxation are localized in cytosol.

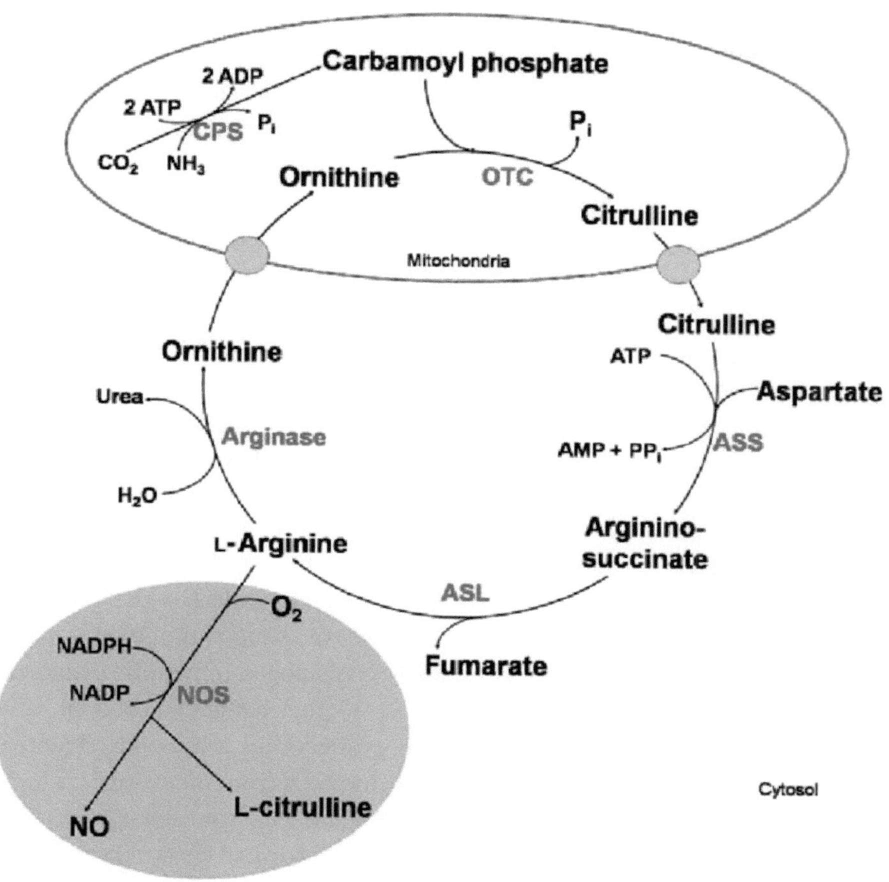

Reactions of urea cycle

Digestion, absorption & metabolism of protein & related disorders

Digestion and Absorption:

The main nutrients in the diet are carbohydrates, proteins and lipids. They are digested and absorbed in the stomach and intestines. Some of the digested / spoiled parts of food items may be reused or removed. Chewing food, movement of the stomach and intestines helps digest food and makes them more susceptible to diarrhea.

Proteolytic enzymes are not present in saliva production, so there is no digestion of protein in the mouth. Proteolysis occurs in the gastro-intestinal tract (i.e. the stomach and intestines). When protein enters the stomach it stimulates the production of a hormone called gastrin which also stimulates the release of HCl by parietal cells in the stomach and pepsinogen from larger cells.

Stomach juice contains acid i.e. pH is 1.5—2.5. Stomach pH acid has an antibacterial action that kills bacteria and other germs. At this pH the dietary protein also undergoes changes. In the presence of HCl, pepsinogen is converted to pepsin by autocatalysis leading to the release of other amino acids from the amino acids. Pepsin is the endopeptidase of tyr, phe, trp.

In the stomach the proteins are converted as follows:

Protein → Metaprotein → Proteone → Peptone → Peptide

As food passes through the stomach to the small intestine the low pH of the diet causes the release of the hormone 'secretin' in the blood. It stimulates the pancreas to release HCO3 in the small intestine to reduce HCl. Intake of HCO3 in the intestine suddenly raises the pH from 2.5 to 7.0. The entry of amino acids into the duodenum releases the hormone 'cholecystokinin' which causes the release of pancreatic juice (which contains many pancreas enzymes such as trypsinogen, chymotrypsinogen, procarboxypeptidase) by exocrine cells of the pancreas (ecbolic and hydrolatic). Most of these enzymes are produced as zymogens (inactive enzymes) by the pancreas to protect exocrine cells from digestion.

After trypsinogen infiltration into the small intestine it begins to act on trypsin with enterokinase secreted by the intestinal cells. Trypsin was synthesized by trypsinogen by releasing hexapeptide at the end of the N-terminal.

Newly developed trypsin activates residual trypsinogen, Trypsin is endopeptidase, which is active (active) in peptide bonds supplied with basic amino acids such as arginine, histidine and lysine. Chymotrypsin is produced in an inactive compound called chypotin chymotrypsinogen. Chymotrypsin is the endopeptidase target for fragrant amino acids namely phenylalanine, tyrosine, tryptophan.

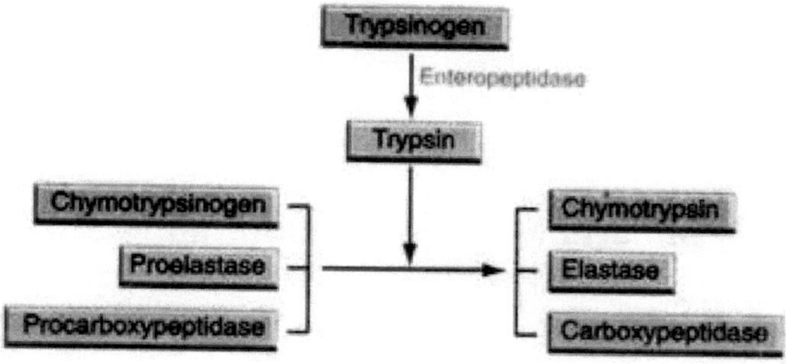

Carboxypeptidase produced as procarboxypeptidase is also activated by trypsin. It is the exopeptidase that breaks down the amino acids at the end of the carboxy. The amino peptidase produced as pro-aminopeptidase is also activated by trypsin. It is the exopeptidase that separates the amino acids into the free amino acids. Dipeptides work only on dipeptides and hydrolyzes into 2 amino acids.

Proteolytic enzymes and their action

Secreted in	Enzymes secreted	Action
Stomach	Pepsin	Converts complex proteins to small peptides
Pancreas	Trypsin	➤ Specifically acts on peptide bonds contributed by basic amino acids like arg, lys & his ➤ Activates trypsinogen to trypsin ➤ Procarboxypeptidase to carboxypeptidase, proelastase to elastase and proaminopeptidase to aminopeptidase
	Chymotrypsin	Specifically acts on peptide bonds contributed by aromatic amino acids like phe, tyr, trp
	Carboxypeptidase	Carboxy terminal amino acids
	Elastase	
Small intestine	Amino peptidase	Amino terminal amino acids
	Dipeptidase	Acts on dipeptides and releases free amino acids

Celiac Disease:

This is a rare disease caused by a deficiency / lack of an enzyme needed to produce proteins containing N-glutamyl amino acids. As a result, intestinal enzymes are unable to digest the insoluble protein in water found in wheat called gliadin which damages cells around the small intestine.

In rare cases the inactive zymogen types of enzymes stored in the pancreas ripen earlier into active forms in the pancreas itself, which may be harmful to the pancreas. Antagonists called a trypsin inhibitor, a pancreas-derived protein can be used to prevent such a disaster.

Biologically important compounds synthesized from various amino acids

1.Ala amino acid

Found in protein in 1875, alanine makes up 30% of silk residues. Its low regeneration contributes to a simple, long silk fabric with a few contrasting links that give the fibers strength, elasticity and flexibility. Only l-stereoisomer participates in protein biosynthesis.

2.Arg amino acid

In humans, arginine is produced when proteins are digested. It can also be converted into nitric oxide by the human body, a chemical known to relax the arteries.

Due to its vasodilatory effects, arginine has been implicated in the treatment of people with chronic heart disease, high cholesterol, impaired blood circulation and high blood pressure, although research into these methods is still ongoing. Arginine can also be synthetically produced, and arginine-related compounds can be used in the treatment of people with liver failure due to its role in promoting liver regeneration. Although arginine is needed for growth but not for bodybuilding, studies have shown that arginine is essential for wound healing, especially for those who have poor circulation .

3.Asn amino acid

In 1806, asparagine was purified with asparagus juice, making it the first amino acid to be separated from the natural source. However, it was not until 1932 that scientists were able to prove that asparagine is a protein.

Only the l-stereoisomer contributes to the biosynthesis of breast proteins. Asparagine is important in removing toxic ammonia from the body.

4.Asp amino acid

Found in protein in 1868, aspartic acid is commonly found in animal proteins, however only l-stereoisomer contributes to protein biosynthesis. Water solubility of these amino acids leads to the presence near active sites of enzymes such as pepsin.

5.Cys amino acid

Cysteine is rich in protein for hair, hooves, and keratin, as separated from urinary calculus in 1810 and from horn in 1899. Next, it was chemically bound, and the structure was completed in 1903-4.

The sulfur-containing thiol group in the cysteine chain is key to its properties, allowing the formation of disulfide bridges between two peptide chains (as in insulin) or loop formation within a single chain, affecting the formation of the final protein. The two cysteine molecules that are bound together by disulfide bonds form the amino acid cystine, which is sometimes listed separately from the normal amino acid sequence. Cysteine is made in the body from serine and methionine and is only present in the l-stereoisomer in mammalian proteins.

People with genetic cystinuria are unable to successfully absorb the cystine in their blood. Thus, high levels of cystine form in their urine where they crystallizes and form stones that block the kidneys and bladder.

6.Gln amino acid

Glutamine was first separated from beetroot juice in 1883, separated from protein in 1932 and then chemically synthesized the following year. Glutamine is the most abundant amino acid in our body and performs many important functions. In humans, glutamine is linked to glutamic acid and this conversion step is especially important in regulating the level of toxic ammonia in the body, creating urea and purines.

7.Glu amino acid

Glutamic acid was separated from wheat gluten in 1866 and chemically synthesized in 1890. It is commonly found in animal proteins, the only l-stereoisomer occurring in mammalian proteins, which humans are unable to synthesize from the common α-ketoglutaric acid. Monosodium salt ll glutamic acid, monosodium glutamate (MSG) is commonly used as a flavor enhancer. The carboxyl side chain of glutamic acid is able to act as a donor and receptor for ammonia, which is toxic to the body, allowing safe transport of ammonia in the liver when converted to urea and excreted by the kidneys. Free glutamic acid can also be reduced to carbon dioxide and water or converted to sugar.

8.Gly amino acid

Glycine became the first amino acid to be separated from the protein, in this case gelatin, and is the only one that does not work visually (no d- or l-stereoisomers). Structurally α-amino acid is very simple, it does not work when combined with protein. However, glycine is essential for the biosynthesis of the amino acid serine, coenzyme glutathione, purines and heme, an important component of hemoglobin.

9.His amino acid

Histidine was disbanded in 1896 and its structure was confirmed by chemical synthesis in 1911. Histidine is a direct precursor to histamine and is also an important source of carbon for purine synthesis. When incorporated into proteins, the histidine chain on the side can act as a proton receptor and donor, transmitting important components when combined with enzymes such as chymotrypsin and those involved in the utilization of carbohydrates, proteins, and nucleic acids.

In infants, histidine is considered an essential amino acid, adults can walk for a short time without eating but it is still considered essential.

10.Ile amino acid

Isoleucine was isolated from beet sugar molasses in 1904. The hydrophobic nature of the isoleucine's side chain is important in determining the high protein composition in which it is incorporated.

Those suffering from a rare hereditary disease called maple syrup urine, have a defective enzyme in the normal breakdown of isoleucine, leucine, and valine. In addition to treatment, metabolites that form in a patient's urine give off a distinct odor that gives the condition its name.

11.Leu amino acid

Leucine was separated from cheese in 1819 and muscle and hair in its shiny condition in 1820. In 1891, it was integrated into a laboratory.

Only l-stereoisomer is derived from the protein of mammals and can be digested into simple compounds with body enzymes. Some DNA binding proteins contain regions in which leucines are arranged in a configuration called leucine zippers.

12.Lys amino acid

Lysine was first isolated from the milk protein casein in 1889, and its composition was clarified in 1902. Lysine is important for binding enzymes to coenzymes and plays a key role in the way histones work.

Many cereal plants have very low lysine which has led to a shortage of other people who rely heavily on this diet and vegetarians as well as a low-fat diet. As a result, efforts have been made to develop lysine-rich maize varieties.

13.Met amino acid

Methionine was isolated from the milk protein casein in 1922, and its formation was resolved by a laboratory compound in 1928. Methionine is an important source of sulfur for many compounds in the body, including cysteine and taurine. Combined with its sulfur, methionine helps prevent fat accumulation in the liver, and it helps in the removal of metabolic waste and toxins.

Methionine is the only essential amino acid that is not in the significant amount of soy beans and is therefore commercially produced and added to many soy products.

14.Phe amino acid

Phenylalanine was first isolated from the natural source (lupine shoots) in 1879 and later chemically synthesized in 1882. The human body is normally able to break down phenylalanine into tyrosine, but in people with genetic phenylketonuria (PKU), the enzyme that causes this conversion is inactive. When left untreated, phenylalanine builds up in the blood and causes cognitive development in children. For every 10,000 babies born with the condition, a diet high in phenylalanine early can alleviate the side effects.

15.Pro amino acid

In 1900, proline was chemically synthesized. The following year this was separated from the milk casein protein and its composition was shown to be similar. Humans can synthesize proline from glutamic acid, which is only seen as an l-stereoisomer in mammalian proteins. When proline is synthesized with proteins, its abnormal formation leads to sharp bends, or kinks, in a series of peptides, which contribute significantly to the final protein structure. Proline and the hydroxyproline extracted from it, make up 21% of the amino-acid residues of fibrous protein collagen, essential for connective tissue.

16.Ser amino acid

Serine was first isolated from the silk protein in 1865, but its structure was not established until 1902. Humans can synthesize serine from other metabolites, including glycine, although only l-stereoisomer is derived from mammalian proteins. Serine is essential for the biosynthesis of many metabolites and is generally responsible for the catalytic activity of the enzymes involved, including chymotrypsin and trypsin.

Nerve gases and other pesticides work in combination with serine residue in the active acetylcholine esterase, which completely inhibits the enzyme. Esterase activity is important in differentiating the neurotransmitter acetylcholine from dangerously high levels of lead, which quickly leads to convulsions and death.

17.Thr amino acid

Threonine was isolated from fibrin in 1935 and synthesized the same year. The only l-stereoisomer that comes from animal proteins in mammals when inactive. Although important for many bacterial responses, its metabolic role in high-dose animals, including humans, remains unclear.

18.Trp amino acid

Separated from casein (milk protein) in 1901, the tryptophan structure was established in 1907, but only l-stereoisomer is derived from mammary proteins. In the human gut, bacteria break down food tryptophan, releasing compounds such as skatole and indole that give the faeces its unpleasant odor. Tryptophan is converted to vitamin B3 (also called nicotinic acid or niacin), but not in sufficient quantity to keep us healthy. So we should also take vitamin B3, a failure to do so that leads to a deficiency called pellagra.

19.Tyr amino acid

In 1846 tyrosine was isolated from the collapse of casein (a protein derived from cheese), after which it was incorporated into a laboratory and its structure determined in 1883. Available only in l-stereoisomer in mammalian proteins, humans can synthesize tyrosine from phenylalanine. . Tyrosine is an important precursor of the adrenal hormones epinephrine and norepinephrine, thyroid hormones including thyroxine and hair and pigment melanin. In enzymes, tyrosine residues are often associated with functional areas, the modification of which can alter the enzyme specificity or completely degrade activity.

Those with genetic phenylketonuria (PKU) are unable to convert phenylalanine into tyrosine, while patients with alkaptonuria have a problem with tyrosine metabolism, which produces a distinct black urine when exposed to air.

20.Val amino acid

The valine structure was established in 1906, after the first division of albumin in 1879. The only l-stereoisomer derived from mammary protein. Valine can be reduced to simple compounds in the body, but in people with a rare genetic condition called maple syrup urine, the wrong enzyme disrupts the process and can be fatal if left untreated.

In born errors of amino acid metabolism – only aromatic amino acids

1. Phenylketonuria (PKU):

PKU occurs due to the dysfunction of the amino acid phenylalanine. Affected children show normal physical growth but mental retardation to a different degree. Untreated children become adults with intellectual disabilities.

Food Management:

a. Clinical symptoms do not occur if the affected baby is put on a diet low in phenylalanine immediately after birth and stored for a long time.

b. Excessive emotional stress is placed on the young child in a completely processed diet.

c. Immediately after diagnosis, breastfeeding should be stopped and the baby should be bottle-fed with a small amount of phenylalanine milk.

d. The greatest difficulty arises when a baby is to be weaned. The mother then prepares for her baby a diet low in phenylalanine in five lists. Therefore, you need ongoing help from a dietitian.

2. Galactosemia:

This genetic factor due to reduced glucose-1 -phosphate uridyl transferase activity interferes with galactose metabolism increasing its concentration in the blood. Toxic symptoms appear immediately after birth when the baby begins to drink milk and is due to the accumulation of galactose-1-phosphate within the cells. This feature is very rare.

Treatment:

a. Breastfeeding should be stopped immediately and the baby should be given a milk powder when lactose is replaced by dextrin, dextrose and maltose.

b. Milk, dairy products and food preparations containing these should be excluded from the diet. It is necessary to keep these limits for life.

c. Consumption of galactosides, which are present in small amounts in many foods, and widely used in the food industry as a filler or flavoring agent, should be reduced.

3. Refsum's Disease:

This is due to a deficiency in the enzyme systems responsible for the conversion of phytanic acid (3, 7, 1, 15-tetramethyl-hexadecanoic acid) that accumulates in plasma and tissues. Phytanic acid is found in phytol, a hydrolysis product of chlorophyll.

Treatment:

a. Significant improvement is possible by removing phytanic acid by plasma exchange and low chlorophyll intake.

b. There should be a ban on too many fruits and vegetables, butter and edible oils.

4. Maple-Syrup Urine Disease:

Deterioration in the oxidative removal of branched-chain amino acids, leucine, isoleucine and valine, leads to the accumulation of its oxidants in the blood and excreted in the urine releasing the aroma of maple syrup.

5. Fructose Intolerance:

Lack of the enzyme aldolase that converts fructose-l-phosphate into dihydroxyacetone phosphate, as well as glyceraldehyde causes the disease. When fructose is absorbed, fructose-l-phosphate accumulates in the liver. This disrupts the release of glucose from the liver and leads to severe hypoglycemia.

6. Von Gierke's Disease:

This is due to a factor in low glucose-6-phosphatase activity in which glycogen can be synthesized and large amounts of fat accumulate in the liver. Most patients survive in adult life from this rare disease.

Treatment:

a. High protein foods speed up gluconeogenesis from amino acids and help maintain blood sugar.

b. In severe cases, it may need to be fed regularly every 3 to 4 hours.

c. A limited amount of carbohydrates is required, but this should be in the form of glucose or starch.

d. Both sucrose and lactose should be avoided, as fructose and galactose are easily converted into glycogen in the liver.

Plasma protein – types, function & normal values

The plasma proteins of human blood are a mixture of simple proteins, glycoproteins, lipoproteins, and other compounds called "Plasma Protein."

Types of Plasma Proteins

The three most important components of plasma proteins are albumin, globulin, and fibrinogen. For satisfactory correction by electrophoresis, these components are classified as follows:

Albumin - 55.2%

α1-Globulin - 5.3% (α1-Antitrypsin, TBG, Transcortin, etc.)

α2-Globulin - 8.6% (Haptoglobulin, ceruloplasmin, α2- macroglobulin, etc.)

B-Globulin - 13.4% (β1-transferrin, β-lipoprotein, etc.)

¥ -Globulin - 11.0% (Immune system, etc.)

Fibrinogen - 6.5%

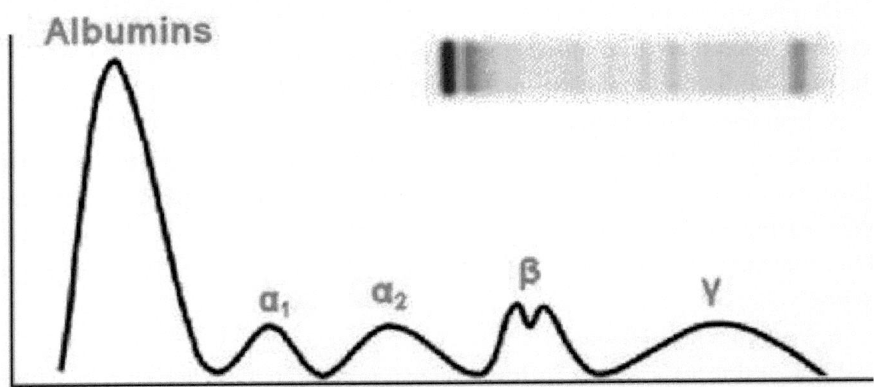

1. Albumin

The most abundant component of plasma protein (2.8 to 4.5 gm / 100 ml) with very high electrophoretic mobility. It dissolves in water and is stimulated by complete ammonium sulfate. Albumin binds to the liver and contains a single polypeptide chain of 610 amino acids weighing 69,000 cells. Serum albumin contains essential amino acids such as lysine, leucine, valine, phenylalanine, threonine, arginine, and histidine. Acidic amino acids such as aspartic acid and glutamic acid are also concentrated in albumin.

These residues make the molecule highly charged for both positive and negative charges. In addition to playing the role of a healthy diet, albumin acts as a transport carrier of various biomolecules such as fatty acids, trace elements, and drugs. Another important function of albumin is to maintain osmotic pressure and to distribute fluid between blood and tissues.

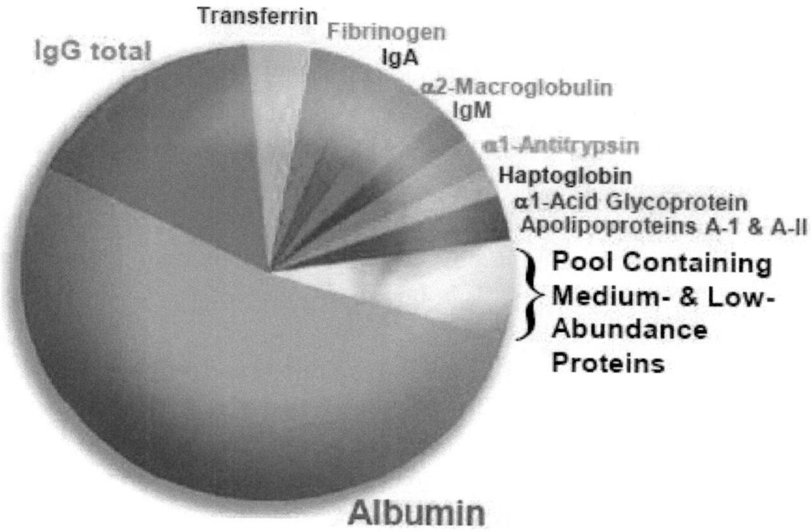

2. Globulins

With electrophoresis, plasma globulins are broken down into α1, α2, β, and ¥ -globulins. These proteins are secreted into the liver, and ¥-gllobulins are produced in the cells of the reticuloendothelial system. The typical serum globulin (concentration) concentration is 2.5 gm / 100 ml (Howe method) or 3.53 gm / 100 ml by electrophoresis.

a. α1-Globulin

This component includes a number of complex proteins that contain carbohydrates and lipids. These are orosomucoid, α1-glycoprotein, and α-lipoprotein. The normal serum α1-globulin level is 0.42 gm / 100 ml. Orosomucoid is rich in carbohydrates, soluble in water, does not burn, and weighs 44,000 cells. It works to transport hexosamine complexes to the muscles. Lipoproteins are soluble compounds that contain non-binding lipids. These proteins act primarily as carriers for transporting different lipids in the body.

b. α2-Globulins

This component also contains complex proteins such as α2-glycoproteins, plasminogen, prothrombin, haptoglobin, ceruloplasmin (transports Cu), and α2-macroglobulin. The normal serum value of this component is 0.67 gm / 100 ml. Plasminogen and prothrombin are precursors of plasmin and thrombin, respectively, and both of these proteins play an important role in blood clotting .

Haptoglobulins are also glycoproteins with a molecular weight of 85,000 cells. These are bound to the liver and can bind to any free hemoglobin that may appear in plasma as a result of erythrocytes 'lysis, thus preventing the release of Hb and its associated iron. Ceruloplasmin is a glycoprotein that binds to the liver and is an important part of the body's copper metabolism. About 95% of plasma copper is bound to this protein.

c. β-Globulins

This fraction of plasma proteins contains these β-lipoproteins, which are rich in lipid content. It also contains transferrin (siderophilin), which transports non-heme iron to plasma. The normal serum value of β-globulins is 0.91 gm / 100 ml. Transferrin is a metal transport protein, and can be supplemented with iron up to 33% in plasma. It has a low carbohydrate content.

d. ¥-Globulins

These are also called Immunoglobulins and have antibody activity. Based on their electrophoretic mobility, they are classified as IgG, IgA, and IgM. Immunoglobulins are important clinical components of globulins and are concerned with "the reaction of the immunological reaction." Lymphocytes from this. Two different types of lymphocytes are involved in the production of immunoglobulin "T-cells of Thymus" and "B-Cells" from the bone marrow. "

3. Fibrinogen

Fibrous protein with a weight of 340,000 cells. It has six polypeptide chains bound together by disulfide bonding. Thrombin converts fibrinogen into fibrin, which plays a key role in blood vessels. In addition to the proteins mentioned above, plasma contains a number of enzymes, such as acid phosphatase and alkaline phosphatase, which have important diagnostic value.

Functions of Plasma Proteins

Plasma proteins are essential for our body. Here are the key functions.

1. Protein Nutrition
2. It acts as a source of protein for muscles whenever the need arises.
3. Osmotic pressure and water balance

4. It has an osmotic pressure of about 25 mm Hg and plays an important role in maintaining proper fluid balance between tissues and blood.
5. Plasma albumin is responsible for this activity primarily due to its low molecular weight and quantity control over other proteins.
6. During the loss of protein in the body, such as kidney disease, excess fluid travels through the tissues, producing edema.
7. Buffer action: -Plasma proteins help maintain body pH by acting as ampholytes. With normal pH of blood, they act as acids and receive captions.

Causes of proteinuria, hypoproteinemia, hyper-gamma globinemia

1.proteinuria

Proteinuria is an increase in protein in the urine. This condition can be a sign of kidney damage. Proteins - which help build muscle and bone, control the amount of fluid in the blood, fight infections and repair tissue - should stay in the blood. When protein enters the urine it eventually leaves the body, unhealthy.

Causes of proteinuria

In most cases, proteinuria is caused by risk factors (non-cancer) or temporary medical conditions.

This includes

- Dehydration
- Inflammation and low blood pressure.
- Excessive exercise or work, emotional stress.
- Aspirin treatment and cold exposure can also cause proteinuria. In addition, kidney stones in the urinary tract can cause proteinuria.

In some cases, proteinuria is the first sign of chronic kidney disease with a gradual loss of kidney function that may eventually require dialysis or kidney transplantation. Diabetes and high blood pressure can damage the kidneys and are the causes of kidney disease.

2.Hypoproteinemia

Hypoproteinemia is a lower protein level than normal in the body.

Protein is an essential nutrient found in almost every part of your body - including your bones, muscles, skin, hair, and nails. Protein keeps your bones and muscles strong. It forms a molecule called hemoglobin, which carries oxygen throughout your body. It also produces chemicals called enzymes, which cause many reactions that keep your organs working.

You get protein from foods like red meat, chicken, fish, tofu, eggs, milk and nuts. You need to eat protein every day, because your body does not keep it.

Lack of protein can cause problems such as:

- Muscle loss
- Slow growth
- The immune system is weak
- Heart and lungs weak
- Severe protein deficiency can be life-threatening.

causes

There are several reasons why your body may be low in protein.

- There is not enough protein in your diet
- You may be deficient in protein if you do not eat enough food sources - for example, if you follow a vegetarian or vegan diet. A severe protein deficiency is called Kwashiorkor. This condition is especially common in developing lands where people do not have enough to eat.
- Your body cannot properly absorb the protein from the food you eat

The problem of absorbing protein from food is called malabsorption. Possible causes include:

- Celiac disease
- Crohn's disease
- Parasites and other diseases
- Damage to your pancreas

- Defects in your gut
- Surgery, which includes weight loss surgery or procedures that remove part of your intestines

- **Liver damage**:- Your liver produces a protein called albumin, which makes up about 60 percent of the total amount of protein in your blood. Albumin carries vitamins, hormones, and other substances throughout your body. It also prevents the fluid from leaking into your bloodstream (which is why fluid builds up in your body if you do not have protein). Damage to your liver prevents us from making albumin.
- **Kidney damage**:-Your kidneys filter the waste products into your bloodstream. When your kidneys are damaged, impurities that need to be filtered remain in your bloodstream. Things like proteins, which need to stay in your bloodstream, leak into your urine. Too much protein in your urine due to kidney damage is called proteinuria.

Hyper-gamma globinemia

Hypergammaglobulinemia is a rare condition that is usually the result of an infection, autoimmune disorder, or malignancy such as multiple myeloma. It is characterized by high levels of immunoglobulins in your blood.

Immunoglobulins are antibodies that circulate in your bloodstream and tissues that work to remove germs, bacteria, fungi, and foreign substances from the blood. There are different types of antibodies in your blood. The most common antibody is Immunoglobulin G (IgG). People with hypergammaglobulinemia often have elevated IgG levels.

Causes of Hypergammaglobulinemia

Since the exact cause of hypergammaglobulinemia is not yet known, any virus, bacteria, fungus, or condition that interferes with normal immune function or immune response may be a possible cause of hypergammaglobulinemia.

Hypergammaglobulinemia may be the result of an autoimmune disease caused by certain diseases, such as:

- Malaria
- Bacterial infections
- Viral infections

Other causes may include:

- Severe infection
- Arthritis
- Multiple myeloma
- Liver disease

There are certain types of hypergammaglobulinemia that are family diseases - a genetic condition that occurs more often in family members than might be expected by chance.

Principle of electrophoresis, normal & abnormal

Electrophoresis

Electrophoresis helped us to find the colloid particles .

When an electric field is applied to all two electrodes completely immersed in a colloidal solution, the particles (colloidal) usually go to one or more electrodes. This movement of particles under the effect of an electric field is known as electrophoresis.

Ferdinand Frederic Reuss became the first man to experience this condition in 1807. The positively charged particles (cations) moving to the cathode were called cataphoresis and the negative particles (anions) moving to the anode were called anaphoresis.

This process is performed in laboratories to perform DNA and RNA analysis. This process uses negative charging to move proteins to good charging.

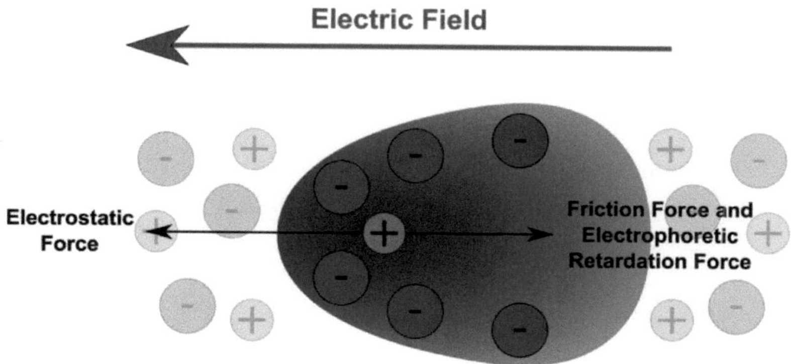

Types of Electrophoresis

We can testify to its various uses in various industries, some of which are:

1. Paper Electrophoresis
2. Agarose Gel Electrophoresis
3. Pulsed Field Electrophoresis
4. Capillary Electrophoresis
5. Microchip Electrophoresis

Electrophoresis used in the Medical Industry are:-

Gel Electrophoresis:

Let explain this with the help of an experiment. We use a small test tube with some clear liquid in it and that liquid contains DNA strands of different lengths.

Let's explain this with the help of experiments. We use a small test tube that contains a specific liquid and that liquid contains strands of DNA of different lengths.

DNA strands can be divided into short, medium, and long strands. The strands of DNA are so tiny that you can't even see them under a microscope, but there is a way to find the strands of DNA without touching or seeing them.

This process is known as Gel electrophoresis. This process also helps to separate molecules like proteins. The gel is like a sponge and has many holes and the gel is used as a filter to separate the DNA strands. There are small holes in the end of the gel and we place DNA samples in these holes. Then, with the help of electric current, we make the DNA move and with the help of the electrophoresis process, we push the strands of DNA through a gel filter.

Longer strands are slower compared to smaller strands in gel holes and cables of the same length will travel at the same speed. In this way the strands of DNA are self-organizing. To make fibers visible to the naked eye, we pollute the organized group of DNA strands.

Protein Electrophoresis:

1. This method is used to calculate the presence of abnormal proteins and the absence of normal proteins and to identify the types of proteins present in high or low levels in the blood. In this process, proteins are divided on the basis of size and electrical charging.
2. Electrophoretic patterns in the normal human pathological and pathological series of plasma and plasma were obtained using the schlieren scanning method. From these patterns the movement and concentration of different protein components electrophoretically is calculated electronically. The movement falls into five well-defined groups associated with albumin, α, β, and γ globulins, as well as fibrinogen. The concentration of different components in the pathological sea has been compared with those in normal sera. As indicated in the information below: -

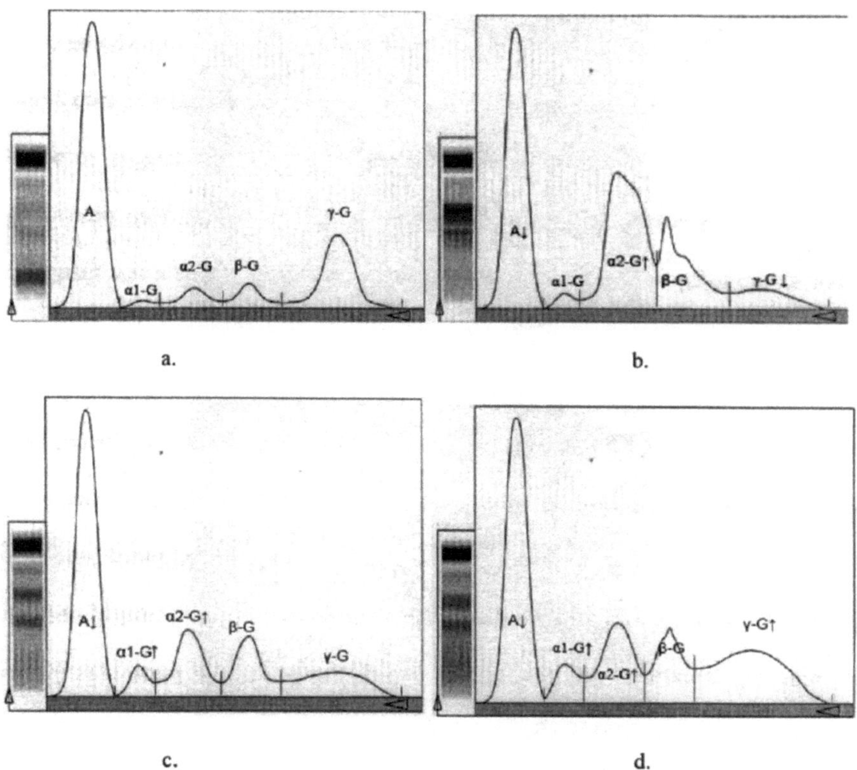

Electrophoretic patterns: a. normal; b. nephrotic syndrome; c. acute inflammatory response; d. chronic inflammatory response

CHAPTER IV

Clinical Enzymology

- Isoenzymes – Definition & properties
- Enzymes of diagnostic importance in
- Liver Diseases-ALT, AST, ALP, GGT
- Myocardial infarction-CK, cardiac troponins, AST, LDH
- Muscle diseases-CK, Aldolase
- Bone diseases-ALP
- Prostate cancer-PSA, ACP

Isoenzymes – Definition & properties

Definition of Isozymes:

Enzymes that come in many different forms and differ from each other chemically, immunologically and electrophoretically are called "Isoenzymes" or "isozymes".

Occurrence of Isozymes:

Isozyme is present in the serum and tissues of mammals, aquatic animals, birds, insects, plants and rare organisms.

Examples:

Isozymes of many dehydrogenases, and several oxidases, transaminase, phosphatase, transphosphorylases, proteolytic enzymes, aldolases.

Characteristics of Isozymes:

1. They make the same reaction but can be differentiated by physical means such as electrophoresis or by immunology methods.

2. The difference between other isozyms is due to differences in the quarterly structure of the enzymes, e.g., lactate dehydrogenase exists in five isozymic pathways.

3. The isozymic types of lactate dehydrogenase are tetramers, each composed of two types of units H and M. The molecular weight of active lactate dehydrogenase is 1,30,000. Only tetrameric molecule has catalytic activity.

4. Separation and reconstruction of lactate dehydrogenase -I1 or lactate dehydrogenase- 15 produces new isozymees. Therefore, each contains one subunit.

But when a mixture of pure lactate dehydrogenase - I1 and lactate dehydrogenase - I5 is subdivided into reconstruction, lactate dehydrogenase - I2, - I3 and I4 are also produced.

Estimated levels of isozymes result when the relationship is:

Lactate dehydro-genase isozyme		Subunits
I_1	...	H H H H
I_2	...	H H H M
I_3	...	H H M M
I_4	...	H M M M
I_5	...	M M M M

The combination of H and M units is controlled by a different genetic loci.

5. Lactate dehydrogenase (LDH) promotes the transfer of two electrons and one hydrogen ion from lactate to NAD:

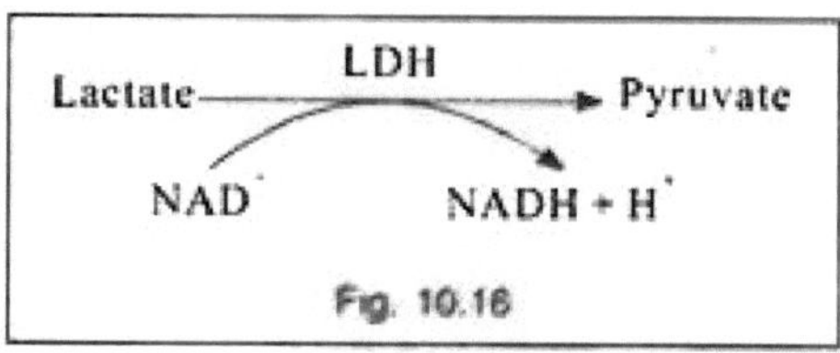

Fig. 10.16

6. Medical discoveries in 1957 showed that the relative dosage of a few isozymes of human lactate dehydrogenase serum was significantly altered in some pathologic conditions.

Enzymes of diagnostic importance

1. Liver Diseases-ALT, AST, ALP, GGT

Liver enzymes

These are chemicals that the liver produces while performing its function of supporting the body's health. An enzyme is a catalyst that assists and strengthens chemical reactions. The body relies on enzymes, many of which are produced by the liver, to allow their chemical processes to work hard enough to support life. Therefore, the liver is a very complex and vital organ, which helps regulate and enhance many different digestive processes and metabolism. The name of the organ comes from the oldest information that is most important in life; means "living thing." Measuring the amount of various liver enzymes in the blood can serve as an important diagnostic tool for diagnosing liver disease, as well as other problems such as kidney disease. For the purposes of blood tests, a small number of large liver enzymes are very important.

Alanine Transaminase (ALT)

Alanine transaminase or ALT is an important liver enzyme for use in diagnosing liver disease, perhaps the single most important enzyme. Significant elevations in ALT levels in the blood indicate damage to the liver cells for a variety of reasons: physical or painful damage to the liver itself, hepatitis (caused by viral or non-viral), diabetes, heart failure, and respiratory problems. bile duct, infectious
mononucleosis, fatty liver disease, and the first symptoms of serious liver problems such as liver failure or liver cancer. Because high ALT can present many different problems, it is always necessary to perform follow-up tests to determine the exact cause of high enzyme and appropriate treatment. Also, ALT levels can vary throughout the day, so a high level of ALT from a single blood test is not a sure sign that something is wrong at all; repeated tests may be indicated to exclude normal diurnal variables.

Aspartate Transaminase (AST)

Aspartate transaminase or AST is another important liver enzyme but is rarely used as an independent test alone. In addition to liver, AST is also found in the heart, skeletal muscles, kidneys, brain, and red blood cells. Therefore, elevated AST is not as obvious a symptom of liver disease as high ALT. High AST may indicate a heart problem and this enzyme is a major heart condition.

The dose of AST to ALT can be used to help diagnose specific liver problems. An AST / ALT rating above 2.0 indicates a risk of developing viral hepatitis, alcohol hepatitis, or liver cancer. If the AST / ALT ratio is between 1.0 and 2.0, it is probably associated with hepatitis. If it is below 1.0, it is likely that there are other liver diseases. Of course, this test is based on the sequence given to the recommended liver enzymes initially.

Alkaline Phosphatase (ALP)

Alkaline phosphatase is an enzyme found in cells that attach to the bile ducts of the liver. Therefore, elevated ALP may indicate obstruction of the bile duct, and other causes of bile can flow from the liver to the duodenum, and other liver diseases. ALP also produces bone and placenta, so it is expected to be elevated in growing children, pregnant women, and elderly patients with Paget's disease, which causes bone loss and degeneration.

Gamma Glutamyl Transpeptidase (GGT)

GGT or gamma glutamyl transpeptidase is actually a much clearer indication of liver disease than ALT. However, it is not used as a first-line test because it may be elevated even with low levels of liver dysfunction which is considered non-clinical (in other words, more sensitive). These tests are often used to determine additional information about a particular liver condition when elevating ALT. GGT is often elevated in chronic alcohol abuse.

2. Myocardial infarction-CK, cardiac troponins, AST, LDH

Cardiovascular enzymes are a broad term that encompasses a few components of intracellular myocytes that can be detected in serum and measured under certain conditions such as myocardial ischemia, trauma, myocarditis. In the appropriate clinical setting, elevated levels of enzymes present in the serum are essential for the diagnosis of myocardial infarction. Although troponin is the most commonly used heart enzyme in the diagnosis of myocardial infarction, others do exist and may be helpful in some cases.

Troponin

Troponin is a regulating protein within the muscle cells involved in the interaction of actin with myosin contractile protein. Troponin I and Troponin T trials are available. Cardiac troponin I is found only in the heart muscle while cardiac troponin T is expressed in very small amounts of skeletal muscle. Contemporary or critical tests for cardiac troponin have been available for years. The most sensitive troponin test is new and first approved for clinical use in 2017. With more sensitive testing, there is a visible troponin range that is considered normal, while this is not the case with older sensitive troponin tests where any height is often considered. important. Troponin assays immunoassays and may give false assumptions about antibody cross-reactivity, although this is rare. Several troponin tests are available, and the levels cannot be compared to all the tests. Older assays can detect troponin levels within 3 to 4 hours of myocardial injury and up to 24 hours. New sensitivity tests detect troponin levels rapidly and vary by trial. Many recommendations based on old experiments recommend repeating troponin doses in 6 to 12 hours, but several techniques are now available in dosage doses immediately after 2 hours.

In most clinical cases, cardiac troponin is the cardiac enzyme of choice, and other enzymes should not be used regularly. There are many reasons for this, but in the end, troponin has been shown to be clear and very sensitive to heart damage. Almost all false troponins are restricted in cases where there is an antibody imbalance within the experimental test, as troponin can be released from the damaged skeletal muscle. CK-MB is removed from the bone marrow, and this can lead to false positives. For each gram of myocardial tissue, more troponin is present than CK-MB.

Creatine Kinase/CK-MB

Creatine kinase is a cytosolic protein involved in the transport of mitochondrial phosphate. CK is present in three different dimer configurations (MM, MB, BB) of the CK two enzymes, M and B. Prior to universal use of troponin, CK-MB was the main heart enzyme for the diagnosis of myocardial infarction.

Creatine kinase is found in all muscle tissue and is not specific to myocyte injury; However, CK-MB is specifically targeted at myocardial tissue. CK-MB can be found in serum within the first 4 to 6 hours of myocardial ischemia; However, it can take up to 12 hours for some patients. CK-MB levels return to baseline within 36 to 48 hours and, therefore, are sometimes used to evaluate recovery after intervention. Elevation of the CK-MB should be interpreted with caution in cases where there is suspected injury or osteoporosis, as CK-MB is released from the injured muscle. Some institutions will report a CK / MB ratio to CK to ensure that the CK-MB height is increased to a greater extent than would be expected from muscle injury alone; however, these measurements or indications were not shown to improve sensitivity or clarity regarding the diagnosis of myocardial ischemia. CK-MB alone levels are very useful in cases where myocardial ischemia is suspected and skeletal muscle injury or disease is not suspected. As discussed below, however, troponin is preferred in almost all cases where it is available for use.

Myoglobin

For many years, CK-MB has been the preferred cardiovascular enzyme for the diagnosis of myocardial ischemia. One problem with this strategy was the length of time from injury to CK-MB elevation. Myoglobin was once used in combination with CK-MB in an effort to accelerate the detection of myocardial injury. Myoglobin is the smallest heme protein found in many tissues. It is released immediately and has a short shelf life. This was a particular advantage when CK-MB was the first trial available; However, as troponin tests have become more sensitive, they have replaced myoglobin to quickly detect myocardial damage. The most sensitive cardiac troponin is released prematurely at the risk of myocardial infarction and is detected in serum before myoglobin.

Heart-Type Fatty Acid Binding Protein

Although not found in the United States, the acid-binding protein of the heart has been shown in one study to be more sensitive than troponin and myoglobin to quickly detect myocardial damage. Troponin was clear; however, the heart-binding acid-binding protein was not studied against the highly sensitive troponin and was not widely accepted for clinical use.

Lactate Dehydrogenase

Previously used in combination with CK-MB, lactate dehydrogenase is also no longer used for the diagnosis of myocardial injury. Lactate dehydrogenase is found in many tissues and is therefore indirect. It also takes a few hours after the onset of the injury to increase levels.

3. Muscle diseases-CK, Aldolase

Aldolase is an enzyme that is involved in glycolysis, which is the process of digesting glucose into energy. Aldolase is mainly found in bone, liver, and brain tissues. High levels of aldolase in the blood arise from muscle diseases including Duchenne muscular dystrophy, dermatomyositis, and polymyositis. High aldolase concentration is not directly related to muscle disease (creatine kinase is very sensitive and clear); However, aldolase may be elevated during muscular dystrophy (myositis) when creatine kinase levels are normal. Aldolase is reported in laboratories as units per liter.

Normal Ranges for aldolase:

0-16 years: <14.5 U/L

> or =17 years: <7.7 U/L

Aldolase is too low

Aldolase levels in the blood cannot be very low. Absence of aldolase in the blood can be considered normal.

Aldolase too high

High blood aldolase levels come from people with Duchenne muscular dystrophy. High levels are also seen in other muscle diseases. Aldolase levels may be very high at the onset of the disease, but only slightly as affected people lose muscle mass. Aldolase may develop temporarily after a heart attack.

Some specific causes of aldolase levels are:

- Duchenne muscular dystrophy
- Dermatomyositis
- Polymyositis
- Leg dystrophy of the legs
- Acute viral hepatitis
- Gangrene
- Prostate tissue
- Trichinosis
- Liver metastases
- Chronic leukemia

Creatine kinase (CK) is an enzyme found mainly in your heart and skeletal muscle, which has small amounts in your brain. Cells from your skeletal muscle, heart muscle, or brain release creatine kinase into your bloodstream when damaged.

An enzyme is a protein that acts as a catalyst to bring about a specific biochemical chemical reaction.

creatine kinase (CK) test

Creatine kinase (CK) testing measures the amount of creatine kinase in your blood.

High CK levels may indicate skeletal muscle, heart or brain damage or deterioration - chronic (long-term) or acute (short-term).

Other names for creatine kinase tests include:

- CK theme.
- CK creatine.
- Phosphokinase CPK.

function of creatine kinase (CK)

The normal activity of creatine kinase (CK) is not really related to the fact that its high levels may indicate blood tests. The function of CK is to add a phosphate group, a collection of natural chemicals, to create, a substance in your muscle cells that helps your muscles produce energy. When CK adds phosphates to creatine, it converts creatine into a highly potent molecule, phosphocreatine, which your body uses to produce energy.

CK enters your bloodstream when muscles, heart or brain experience significant damage or permanent damage. When your muscles are damaged, muscle cells rupture, and their contents, including creatine kinase, leak into your bloodstream.

creatine kinase (CK) tests uses

Healthcare providers often use creatine kinase (CK) tests to diagnose and monitor the following muscle problems:

- Muscle diseases.
- Muscle injury.
- Muscle inflammation (myositis).

Since muscle-related symptoms can be symptoms of several different conditions, your provider may order further tests and CK tests, including:

- Electrolytes.
- BUN (urea blood nitrogen).
- Creatinine.
- Urine myoglobin.

Normal creatine kinase (CK) levels

In a healthy adult, normal creatine kinase (CK) levels can vary due to a few factors, including your:

Gender.

Race.

Activity level.

Ranges also vary from lab to lab due to different test methods. Always check the given reference range on your lab report test results. The normal creatine kinase (CK) ranges are generally higher in people assigned male at birth than in people assigned female at birth.

People who have greater muscle mass normally have higher CK levels than those who don't.

In a healthy adult, normal levels of creatine kinase (CK) may vary due to a number of factors, including yours:

- Gender.
- Race.
- Activity level.

Scope also varies from lab to lab due to different test methods. Always check the scope of reference provided in your lab report test results. The normal range of creatine kinase (CK) is generally higher in males than in females at birth.

People with large muscles often have higher CK levels than those who do not.

High level of creatine kinase (CK)

Having a high level of creatine kinase (CK), or an increase in levels on subsequent CK tests, usually indicates that you have experienced recent muscle damage. CK tests cannot identify any muscle (s) or cause of damage.

Healthcare providers usually receive multiple CK tests to check the progress of your levels. If you have a lot of test results that go up and start to go down, it usually means that your muscle damage is reduced. If your CK levels increase or stay high continuously, it may indicate that you have continuous muscle damage or muscle wasting.

If your results show that you have higher CK levels than usual, your provider may order tests to test specific CK enzyme levels to determine the type of muscle affected, including:

- **CK-MM enzymes:** High levels of CK-MM may indicate that you have muscle damage or disease, such as muscular dystrophy or rhabdomyolysis.
- **CK-MB Enzymes:** High levels of CK-MB may indicate that you have inflammation of your heart muscle or have heart disease or have recently had a heart attack.
- **CK-BB enzymes:** High CK-MB levels may indicate that you have had a stroke or brain injury.

4. Bone diseases-ALP

Alkaline phosphatase (ALP)

It is an enzyme found naturally in your entire body. It comes in many forms called isoenzymes. Each ALP isoenzyme is different, depending on where it is made in your body.

Your bones produce an isoenzyme called ALP-2. The levels of this enzyme increase as your bones grow or bone cells work.

Examination of the bone isoenzyme ALP can detect abnormal bone growth rates that may be associated with conditions such as:

- Paget's arthritis
- bone cancer
- osteoporosis

Other test terms for ALP bone enzymes include:

- ALP-2 testing
- testing of alkaline phosphatase in a particular bone marrow
- bone-specific ALP tests

purpose

Symptoms of arthritis include:

- chronic pain in the bones and joints
- bones break easily or break easily
- bones paralyzed
- ALP-2 tests can also be used to monitor the treatment of arthritis.

Normal values

The ALP bone enzyme range in healthy adults is 12.1 to 42.7.

Children have higher levels of ALP bone enzyme. ALP-2 is also elevated in people with broken bones. In both groups, bone growth is expected and normal.

Higher levels of ALP bone isoenzyme can indicate arthritis such as:

- osteoblastic bone tissue
- osteomalacia, or rickets

- osteoporosis

Paget's disease of bone

A high test result may also indicate serious conditions such as hyperparathyroidism or leukemia. Both of these diseases affect your bones and other parts of your body.

Less than normal test results are sometimes found in people who are malnourished or have anemia. Less common side effects can be found in women taking estrogen after menopause. However, higher levels are more common than low levels.

Prostate cancer-PSA, ACP

PSA

1. Prostate Specific Antigen, or PSA, is an enzyme found in the blood of a man that is only produced by prostate cells. An abnormal increase in PSA, may indicate prostate cancer. High levels of PSA can be found in the blood as prostate cancer cells begin to multiply uncontrollably.

2. Normal PSA levels in the blood are very small doses between 0-2.5 ng / ml. As a man grows his prostate may become larger, leading to slightly higher normal levels of PSA. It is important to have your PSA and prostate examination as part of your annual body.

3. A PSA test requires a man's blood drawn and sent to a laboratory for analysis. If higher levels are obtained than normal, action is recommended. Doses above 2.5 ng / ml, can have many different causes. Prostate Cancer is one of the causes. But high PSA levels do not mean prostate cancer. PSA may also arise due to adverse, non-cancerous conditions such as prostate enlargement, bladder inflammation, infection, or trauma.

Acid phosphatase (ACP)

Definition

Acid phosphatase is a hydrolytic enzyme produced by various cells. Carcinoma from prostatic tissue will have the ability to produce the acid phosphatase enzyme.Aid acid phosphatase has a proper function of less than 7 pH. Prostatic ACP has excellent performance at pH range 5 to 6. ACPs are not stable at temperatures above 37 ° C and above 7.0.

Biochemical features:

- Acid phosphatase (ACP) is present in lysosomes, with the exception of RBCs. Extralysosomal ACP is also present in many cells.
- Acid phosphatase enzyme
- Acid phosphatase contains five isoenzymes.
- Excessive ACP activity occurs in the liver, spleen, milk, RBCs, bone marrow, platelets, and prostate glands.
- The prostate is the richest source of ACP. And it is found in man.
- Osteoclast is a source of increased ACP in growing children compared to adults.

Clinical significance of Acid phosphatase:

1. Osteoclasts are a source of ACP in growing children compared to adults.
2. This is used to diagnose or monitor prostatic carcinoma.
3. A slight or moderate increase in ACP is seen in Paget's disease.
4. In hyperparathyroidism with bone involvement, ACP is elevated.
5. It is recommended when a tumor enters the bone, such as breast cancer.

ACP is raised in:

- Osteoclastoma (a large cell tumor).
- Osteoclastic tissue.
- Osteop Petrosis (marble bone disease).
- Hary-cell leukemia indicates a type of osteoclastic ACP.

CHAPTER V

Acid base maintenance

Acid base maintenance

- pH - definition, normal value
- Regulation of blood pH – blood buffer, respiratory & renal
- ABG – normal values
- Acid base disorders –types, definition & causes

pH - definition, normal value

PH is defined as the negative logarithm of H + ion concentration. The meaning of the word pH is therefore appropriate as hydrogen energy.The normal blood pH of a healthy person ranges from 7.35 to 7.45.

pH Chemistry

The pH scale is a tool for measuring acids and bases. Scale from 0-14: Litmus paper is an indicator used to indicate whether an object is an acid or a base. The color of the paper corresponds to the numbers on the pH scale to indicate the type of object being tested. For example, Vinegar is acidic and measures 2.4 in pH.

A healthy pH balance plays an important role in your overall health, and doctors and scientists often agree on this. The pH level, or possible level of hydrogen, in your body is determined by the type of food and drink you drink. PH concentration of hydrogen ions. This figure is based on a scale from 0 to 14.

pH of Acids and Bases

Here, we have mentioned some of the most important rules when using the pH scale. Students should go through the guidelines provided below to find out more about the similarities.

Neutral Materials have a pH 7 Easy: Neutral solutions have a pH 7. Clean water is neutral. Thus, the pH of pure water is 7. A substance with pH 7 will not affect litmus paper or any other common indicators such as methyl orange or phenolphthalein, etc.

Acids have a pH of Less than 7: A solution with a pH below 7 is an acidic solution. For example, a solution with 4pH will be naturally acidic. The pH 11 solution is more acidic than the other pH 4.4 solution. In other words, the solution of pH 11 will be more potent than any other acid with a pH of 4.4. Solutions with a pH of 0,1,2,30,1,2,3 are often considered strong acids, and solutions with a pH of 4,5,6,4,5,6 are considered weak acid solutions. Solutions with a pH below 7 are naturally acidic, which is why they turn the litmus blue to red. They also turn the methyl orange index red.

Bases have a pH of more than 7: A solution with a pH above 7 is a basic solution or alkaline solution. For example, a solution with a pH of 1111 would be a natural foundation. A solution of pH 14 will be more basic than another solution of pH 1010. In other words, a solution of pH 14 will be a much stronger foundation than another solution of pH 10.10. Solutions with pH values of 8.9, and 10 are generally considered weak foundations, and solutions with pH values of 11,12,13 and 14 are generally considered solid foundations. All substances with a pH above 7 are naturally basic, which is why they turn red litmus into blue. They also respond to phenolphthalein indicator pink.

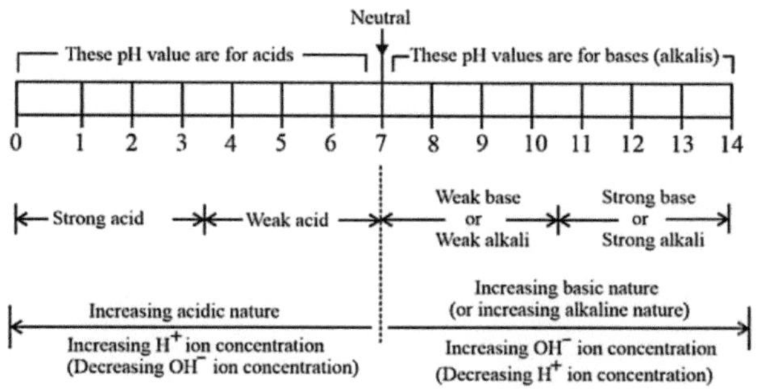

Regulation of blood pH – blood buffer, respiratory & renal

Blood pH Regulation

Blood has the ability to withstand small changes in pH, a condition known as “buffering”. This is due to the basic levels of bicarbonate and hydrogen ions in the blood. Chemical reactions are provided by:

$$CO_2 + H_2O \rightleftarrows H_2CO_3 \rightleftarrows HCO_3^- + H^+$$

CARBON DIOXIDE + WATER — CARBONIC ACID — BICARBONATE + HYDROGEN ION

Chemical Reaction

This reaction can be used to control the pH, as will be discussed in the next section. For example, in active metabolic tissues, there is an increase in hydrogen ions. These can then react with bicarbonate in red blood cells to form carbon dioxide that can be excreted by the lungs. The immune system relies on these statistics. This will be discussed further in due course.

Respiratory Responses

There is a complex control mechanism to change the breathing rate. Chemoreceptors detect certain levels of certain molecules in the blood, and they regulate respiration accordingly. Peripheral chemoreceptors, in the carotid sinus and aortic arch, signal in the brain stem with cranial nerves to change respiratory rate. Intermediate chemoreceptors work differently. If there is an increase in carbon dioxide in the blood, it can spread to cerebrospinal fluid as a small molecule. An enzyme called Carbonic Anhydrase may convert carbon dioxide and water into bicarbonate and hydrogen ions. Hydrogen ions are then exposed to chemical chemoreceptors that alter respiration directly.

Clinical Relevance

Respiratory Acidosis

Respiratory acidosis is an increase in carbon dioxide in the blood, the cause of which is a respiratory system disorder. Common causes include opiates-related respiratory depression, polio-related respiratory disorders and respiratory disorders such as insomnia. This violates the bathing systems and causes a decrease in pH. Therefore, the kidneys should release more hydrogen ions (in the ways discussed earlier) in addition to the increased absorption of bicarbonate.

Respiratory Alkalosis

Respiratory alkalosis is associated with hyperventilation, which can occur as a result of hypoxaemia from the upper extremities or pulmonary embolism. Compensatory mechanisms of respiratory alkalosis are contraindicated in respiratory acidosis. Due to the high levels of bicarbonate, hydrogen ions were re-introduced to try to lower the pH by reducing hydrogen emissions and reducing bicarbonate re-absorption and production.

Acid- Base Balance

Our body maintains a normal pH with an acid-base balance. It is important to maintain homeostasis.

There are various factors that regulate blood pH. The pH of blood plasma depends on CO2, electrolyte and the concentration of weak acid. The two main organs that regulate blood pH are:

Lungs - They are in the gas exchange and remove CO2. The brain regulates the respiratory system so that the brain and lungs maintain blood pH by controlling their speed and energy.

Kidneys - Maintain pH balance by releasing excretion. They remove excess acid or bases that are present in the blood.

Therefore, our body maintains a pH balance through respiration, excretion and other metabolic functions. Any change in the pH of the blood, i.e. acidosis or alkalosis is due to the dysfunction of these organs.

Causes of Abnormal blood pH

Excessive or very low pH is an indication of the malfunction of certain organs. Acidosis or alkalosis is mainly caused by dysfunction of the lungs or kidneys. Any changes in blood pH can be caused by a variety of diseases such as diabetes, poisoning, infection, heart, lung or kidney disease.

High Blood pH

- High blood pH or alkalosis occurs when blood pH is higher than normal. It may be due to a temporary illness or some other serious condition.
- High blood pH may be due to the following reasons:
- Excessive fluid loss such as excessive urination, vomiting, diarrhea, etc.
- When the kidneys do not remove excess alkaline substances from the blood.

Low Blood pH

There are various causes of acidosis and they are more common than alkalosis. The main causes of acidosis include:

- Ketoacidosis in diabetes.
- Metabolic acidosis due to kidney disease or failure.
- Respiratory acidosis due to lung diseases such as pneumonia, respiratory tract infections, asthma, chronic lung diseases.

Therefore, normal pH of blood is essential for normal body function. High or low pH is not a disease in itself but it is due to certain problems. It is an important key to early detection of disease.

ABG – normal values

Arterial blood gas (ABG) test is a diagnostic test done on blood drawn from arteries that give a glimpse of how much oxygen and carbon dioxide in your blood, as well as the pH level of your blood. ABG tests are used to assess respiratory and kidney function and provide a complete overview of the body's immune system.

Purpose of Test

All the cells in your body need oxygen to survive. Inhaling and exhaling air brings oxygen to your body and releases carbon dioxide — a process called gas exchange. However, certain conditions may contribute to this, leading to imbalances in all body systems.

- Shortness of breath
- Breathing hard
- Confusion
- Dizziness
- Nausea

Your healthcare provider may also order an ABG test if you have sleep apnea, heart condition, kidney problems, asthma, cystic fibrosis, chronic obstructive pulmonary disease (COPD), or other conditions that affect breathing and lung function.

ABG can also be a useful metaphor for determining the effectiveness of certain therapies and treatments, such as extra oxygen or medication.

ABG Assesses

In total, the ABG test measures five different markers:

- **Partial pressure of oxygen (PaO2)**: The concentration of oxygen dissolved in the blood (measuring how oxygen can flow from the lungs to the blood).
- **Partial pressure of carbon dioxide (PaCO2):** The pressure of carbon dioxide dissolved in the blood (measuring how carbon dioxide can be excreted from the body).
- **Arterial blood pH,** the amount of hydrogen ions in the blood: A pH of 7.35-7.45 is considered normal.
- **Blood oxygen saturation (SaO2):** The amount of oxygen carried by hemoglobin in red blood cells.
- **Bicarbonate (HCO3):** A chemical lubricant that helps stabilize blood pH.

Normal ABG values fall within the following ranges:

1. Partial pressure of oxygen (PaO2) 75 to 100 millimeters of mercury (mmHg)
2. Partial pressure of carbon dioxide (PaCO2) 35 to 45 mmHg
3. pH7.35 to 7.45
4. Air Completion (SaO2) 95% to 100%
5. Bicarbonate (HCO3) 22 to 26 milliequivalents liter (mEq / liter)

Acid base disorders –types, definition & causes

Normal blood pH is limited to a very low range of 7.35 to 7.45. A person with a blood pH below 7.35 is considered acidosis (literally, "body acidosis," because blood does not really contain acid until its pH drops below 7), and a continuous blood pH under 7.0 can be fatal. Acidosis has a few symptoms, including headaches and confusion, and a person can become weak and easily tired. A person with a blood pH above 7.45 is considered alkalosis, and a pH above 7.8 is fatal. Other symptoms of alkalosis include mental retardation (which may progress to fainting), numbness or numbness in the extremities, muscle spasms and stinging, and nausea and vomiting. Both acidosis and alkalosis can be caused by metabolic disorders or respiratory failure.

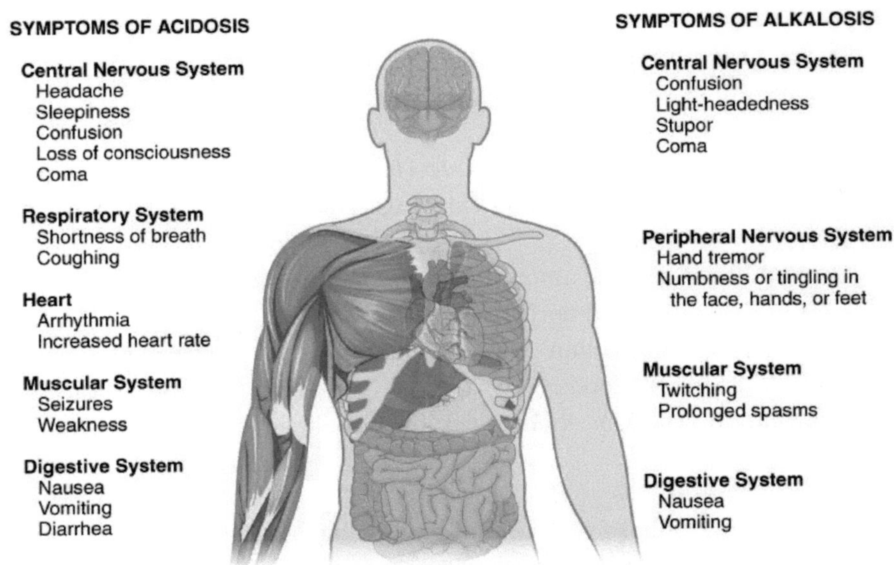

Symptoms of acidosis affect several organ systems. Both acidosis and alkalosis can be diagnosed using a blood test.

Metabolic Acidosis: Primary Bicarbonate Deficiency

Metabolic acidosis occurs when the blood is too acidic (pH below 7.35) due to very low bicarbonate, a condition called primary bicarbonate deficiency. At a normal pH of 7.40, the ratio of bicarbonate and carbonic acid buffer is 20: 1. If a person's blood pH drops below 7.35, it means he is in metabolic acidosis. The most common cause of metabolic acidosis is the presence of organic acids or ketones in the blood. Table 1 lists some of the causes of metabolic acidosis.

Metabolic Alkalosis: Primary Bicarbonate Excess

Metabolic alkalosis is the opposite of metabolic acidosis. Occurs when blood is highly alkaline (pH above 7.45) due to high bicarbonate (called excess bicarbonate overload).

Temporary overdose of bicarbonate in the blood may follow the introduction of excessive amounts of bicarbonate, citrate, or antacids into conditions such as stomach acid — known as heartburn. Cushing's disease, which is a chronic hypersecretion of adrenocorticotrophic hormone (ACTH) by the anterior pituitary gland, can cause chronic metabolic alkalosis. Excessive ACTH overdose causes high aldosterone levels and a steady decrease in potassium through urine excretion. Other causes of metabolic alkalosis include loss of hydrochloric acid in the stomach due to vomiting, decreased potassium due to the use of antihypertensive drugs, and excessive use of laxatives.

Respiratory Acidosis: Primary Carbonic Acid/CO2 Excess

Respiratory acidosis occurs when the blood is too acidic due to the saturation of carbonic acid, which is caused by too much CO2 in the blood. Respiratory acidosis can be the result of anything that interferes with breathing, such as pneumonia, emphysema, or congestive heart failure.

Respiratory Alkalosis: Primary Carbonic Acid/CO2 Deficiency

Respiratory alkalosis occurs when the blood is extremely alkaline due to a lack of carbonic acid and CO2 levels in the blood. This condition usually occurs when too much CO2 is released into the lungs, as is the case with hyperventilation, which is deeper or more frequent than normal. High respiratory rate leading to excessive ventilation may be due to extreme emotional irritability or fear, fever, illness, hypoxia, or unusually high levels of catecholamines, such as epinephrine and norepinephrine. Surprisingly, an overdose of aspirin — a salicylate poison — can cause respiratory alkalosis as the body tries to compensate for its initial acidosis.

Compensation Mechanisms

There are a variety of compensation methods available to maintain blood pH within a limited range, including buffers, respirators, and kidney systems. Although compensation methods are usually very effective, when one of these methods does not work well (such as kidney failure or respiratory disease), they have their limitations. If the ratio of pH and bicarbonate to carbonic acid changes too much, the body may not be able to compensate. In addition, severe changes in pH can create protein. Severe protein damage in this way can lead to disruption of normal metabolic processes, severe tissue damage, and eventually death.

Respiratory Compensation

Respiratory compensation for metabolic acidosis increases respiration rate to release CO2 and converts bicarbonate levels into carbonic acid to 20: 1 levels. This fix is possible in a few minutes. The respiratory compensation for metabolic alkalosis is not as effective as its compensation for acidosis. The normal reaction of the respiratory system to a higher pH is to increase the amount of CO2 in the blood by reducing the respiratory rate to maintain CO2. There is a limit to the reduction of breathing, however, the body can tolerate it. Therefore, the respiratory tract is less effective in compensating metabolic alkalosis than acidosis.

Metabolic Compensation

Metabolic and renal compensation for respiratory diseases that can cause acidosis revolves around the storage of bicarbonate ions. In cases of respiratory acidosis, the kidneys increase bicarbonate retention and H + release through the aforementioned exchange mechanism. These processes increase bicarbonate levels in the blood, and also establish a concentration of bicarbonate and carbonic acid. In cases of respiratory alkalosis, the kidneys reduce bicarbonate production and re-absorb H + into the fluid. These processes can be regulated by the exchange of potassium by kidney cells, which use the K + H + (antiporter) exchange method.

CHAPTER VI

Heme catabolism

Heme catabolism

- Heme degradation pathway
- Jaundice – type, causes, urine & blood investigations (van denberg test)

Heme degradation pathway

Heme Degradation

1. Hemes are cyclic tetrapyrroles that contain iron and are commonly found as an artificial group of hemoglobin, myoglobin and cytochromes.
2. This component of a small globin molecule, essential for the transport of oxygen among other functions is responsible for the complex process of metabolism and degeneration.
3. About 80% of the heme intended for degradation and excretion from yellow erythrocytes is around 3 months.
4. Another 20% is released from erythrocytes prematurely in the bone marrow that are destroyed before they are released into the bloodstream and a small portion is found in other types of cells.

Location of Heme Degradation

Various stages of heme degeneration occur in cells of the reticuloendothelial system, liver, and intestines.

Substrates: Heme; NADPH; 2 UDP-glucuronic acid.

product: Urobilinogen (excreted in urine); stercobilin (extracted from water); carbon monoxide (CO); Fe 2+.

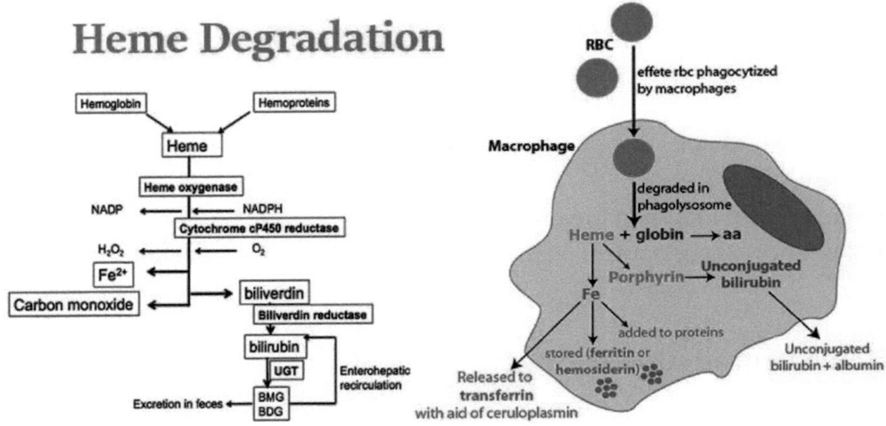

1. Deterioration begins within the spleen macrophages, removing old and damaged erythrocytes (senescent) from circulation.

2. RBCs are covered by cells of the reticuloendothelial system. Globin is further broken down into amino acids, which are further synthesized into cyclic acid cycles and fatty acid oxidation.

3. Heme is oxidized; a heme ring is opened by heme oxygenase. Oxidation occurs in certain carbon, producing linear tetrapyrrole biliverdin, ferric iron (Fe 3+), and CO.

4. In the subsequent reaction, the second methylene compound is reduced by biliverdin reductase, producing bilirubin. So the green color is converted to red-orange bilirubin.

5. Bilirubin is then transferred to the serum via albumin to the liver, where it is combined with glucuronate via bilirubin glucuronyl transferase and excreted in the bile.

6. In the gut, bilirubin is excreted and converted to urobilinogen and stercobilin.Other urobilinogen is also absorbed and excreted as urobilin in the urine. Most urobilinogen is oxidized in the wild to stercobilin which gives the faeces its color.

Significance of Heme Degradation

- Free heme concentration greater than 1 micro M may be toxic because it stimulates the production of active oxygen species. To deal with this problem, heme degeneration is very important in the body.
- In animals, this process is a system of bleeding in which heme from hemoglobin of aging red blood cells, and other hemoproteins, is released from the body.
- Decomposition products such as CO act as a cellular messenger and act on vasodilation. Other heme metabolites also have additional important functions and are involved in a variety of important cellular events.
- Heme depletion is believed to be the evolutionary response to oxidative stress.
- In higher plants, heme is depleted of phycobiliprotein phytochrome which is involved in coordinating light responses.
- In algae, it is converted into a light-harvesting pigment phycocyanin and phycoerythrin.

Jaundice – type, causes, urine & blood investigations (van denberg test)

Jaundice

Jaundice is a disease that causes yellowing of the skin, sclerae (white part of the eye) and mucous membranes. Additionally, body fluids may turn yellow. Technically, it is also called icterus.

It is **caused** by the accumulation of bilirubin in the blood and body tissues. Bilirubin is a waste produced when red blood cells break down. It is then transported to the liver by blood pressure where it is mixed with a digestive fluid called bile.

Normally, bilirubin is excreted in the stool and the rest is excreted in the urine. But when bilirubin cannot be transported to the liver, it builds up in the blood and causes Jaundice.

Causes and Symptoms of Jaundice

Jaundice is more common in newborns and is called neonatal jaundice. This is mainly due to the fact that the liver of the newborn is not fully developed and is not effective in processing bilirubin in the blood.

Types of Jaundice

Jaundice can be divided into three categories. Treatment of jaundice depends on its cause. In other words, treatment directs the symptoms rather than the disease itself.

1. **Hepatocellular jaundice:** Occurs due to injury or damage to the liver. The liver is often damaged by disease, excessive alcohol consumption, and by bacterial infections.
2. **Treatment of Hepatocellular jaundice:** This can be treated with liver transplantation or liver transplantation. The purpose of treatment is to control other damage.
3. **Hemolytic Jaundice:** Occurs when erythrocytes or red blood cells break down rapidly, leading to the formation of extra bilirubin. This is due to infectious diseases such as malaria, anemia etc.
4. **Treatment of Hemolytic Jaundice:** This can be treated by treating a specific cause.
5. **Obstructive Jaundice**This occurs when bilirubin is blocked and can be excreted from the liver.
6. **Treatment for Obstructive Jaundice:** Surgery is performed to remove blockages and clear the bile duct system. Surgery involves removing the gall bladder or part of the bile duct system.

Jaundice Symptoms

Here are some common symptoms of jaundice:

1. Skin color and sclerae turn yellow
2. The color of the urine also changes to yellow
3. Skin itching
4. Fever
5. Abdominal pain
6. Vomiting
7. Weight loss
8. Drowsiness, agitation, and confusion

The color of the skin and the sclera of the eyes turn yellow within a day or two. It is always a good idea to check if the baby has jaundice by gently pressing the baby's chin. If the color changes to yellow for a few seconds, it is suspected that the child is suffering from jaundice.

Additional jaundice symptoms that can be observed in infants are

- Crying out loud

- Change skin tone
- Malnutrition
- The color of the urine turns yellow
- Sleep and fatigue

Blood investigation van denberg test

- Van den Berghreaction is a chemical reaction used to measure bilirubin levels in the blood. Specifically, it determines the amount of bilirubin included in the blood. The reaction produces azobilirubin.
- **Principle:** bilirubin reacts with diazotised sulphanilic acid to produce azobilirubin-purple. This reaction is very helpful in understanding the nature of jaundice. This was initiated by a Dutch physician, Abraham Albert Hijmans van den Bergh (1869–1943) of Utrecht. This test helps identify the type of jaundice. Patient serum is mixed with diazo reagent.
- When red color grows rapidly it is called direct positive. Occurs when conjugated bilirubin is present. In indirect tests, the patient's serum is first treated with alcohol and later combined with diazo reagent. This causes the red color to grow. It is evident when uncontrolled bilirubin is present. When both combined and unbound bilirubin are present, the reaction is called a biphasic reaction.

CHAPTER VII

Organ function tests

Organ function tests (biochemical parameters & normal values only)

- Renal
- Liver
- Thyroid

Renal function test

Kidney Function test:-

The kidneys play a vital role in maintaining your health. One of their most important tasks is to filter out waste products from the bloodstream and excrete them as urine. The kidneys also help control the amount of water and various essential minerals in the body. In addition, they are important in production:

1. Vitamin D
2. Red blood cells
3. Hormones that control blood pressure

Symptoms of kidney problems

Signs that may indicate a problem with your kidneys include:

1. High blood pressure
2. Blood in the urine
3. Quick urination
4. Difficulty starting to urinate
5. Painful urination
6. Swelling of the hands and feet due to the accumulation of fluid in the body

Types of kidney function tests

1.Urinalysis

Urinalysis checks the presence of protein and blood in the urine. There are many possible causes of protein in your urine, not all of which are related to the disease. Infection increases urinary protein, but also strenuous exercise.

Serum creatinine test

This blood test checks that creatinine is growing in your blood. The kidneys often filter the creatinine from the bloodstream. High creatinine levels raise kidney problems.

According to the National Kidney Foundation (NKF), a creatinine level above 1.2 milligrams / deciliter (mg / dL) for women and 1.4 mg / dL for men is a symptom of kidney failure.

Blood urea nitrogen (BUN)

Blood urea nitrogen (BUN) test also looks for waste in your bloodstream. The BUN test measures the amount of nitrogen in the blood. Urea nitrogen is a product of protein degradation.

However, not all high BUN tests result in kidney damage. Ordinary drugs, including large doses of aspirin and other antimicrobials, may increase your BUN. It is important to tell your doctor about any medications or supplements you take regularly. You may need to stop taking certain drugs for a few days before the test.

The standard BUN level is between 7 and 20 mg / dL. A high rate may raise a number of different health problems.

Estimated GFR

This test measures how well your kidneys filter waste. Tests determine quality by looking at factors, such as:

test results, especially creatinine levels

- Age
- Sex
- Race
- Height
- Weight
- Any effect of less than 60 milliliters / minute / 1.73m2 may be a warning sign of kidney disease.

How the tests are performed

- Kidney function tests usually require a 24-hour urine sample and blood test.

- A 24-hour urine sample. A 24-hour urine sample for creatinine clearance test. It gives your doctor an idea of how much creatinine your body produces in one day.

On the day you start the test, urinate in the toilet as you usually do when you wake up.

Night and day, urinate in a special container provided by your doctor. Keep the container closed and refrigerated during collection. Make sure you label the container clearly and tell other family members why we are in the fridge.

On the morning of the second day, you urinate in a container when you wake up. This completes the 24-hour collection process.

Blood samples

A blood drawing specialist first straps an elastic band around your upper arm. This makes the arteries stand out. The technician then cleans the area over the vein. They insert an empty needle into your skin and veins. The blood will flow back to the test tube which will be sent for analysis.

You may feel a sharp tingling or tingling as the needle goes into your arm. The specialist will place a gauze and bandage over the piercing area after the test. The area around the piercing may be damaged in the next few days. However, you should not feel too much or too little pain.

Liver Function test

Liver function tests A blood test used to help diagnose and monitor liver disease or damage. Tests measure the levels of certain enzymes and proteins in your blood.

One of these tests measures the liver's ability to perform its normal function of protein production and the release of bilirubin, a blood clot. Other liver function tests measure the enzymes released by liver cells as a result of injury or diagnosis.

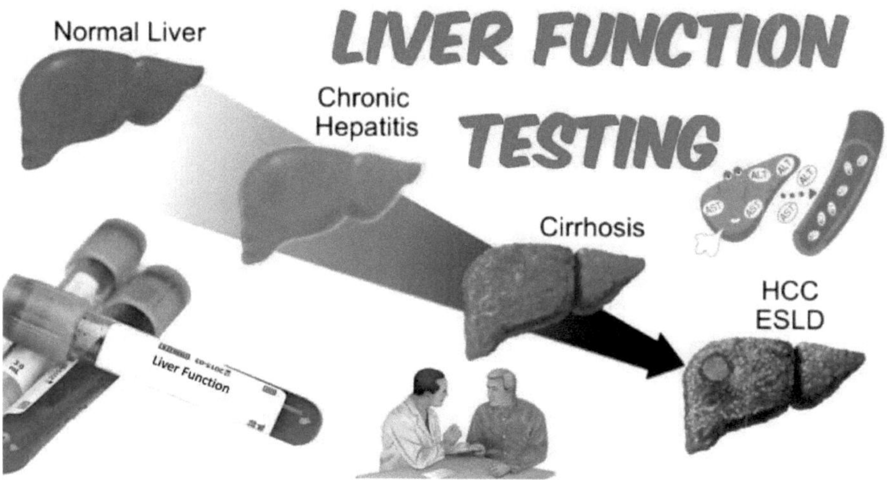

Liver Function Test

Liver function tests check the levels of certain enzymes and proteins in your blood. Higher or lower levels than usual may indicate liver problems. Other common liver function tests include:

1. Alanine transaminase (ALT). ALT is an enzyme found in the liver that helps convert proteins into liver cells. When the liver is damaged, ALT is released into the bloodstream and levels increase.ALTU tests A higher result than normal in this test can be a sign of liver damage. Extremely high levels of more than 1,000 units (U / L) are usually caused by viral hepatitis, ischemic hepatitis, or damage to drugs or other chemicals. ALT of more than 25 units per liter (IU / L) for women and 33 IU / L for men usually requires further testing and evaluation.

2. Aspartate transaminase (AST). AST is an enzyme that helps digest amino acids. Like ALT, AST is usually present in the blood at low levels. Increased AST levels may indicate liver damage, disease or muscle damage. ASTU testing A high result in AST tests may indicate a problem with your liver or muscles. High AST in addition to high ALT may indicate heart or muscle disease. When ALT, bilirubin, and ALP are also elevated, they may indicate liver damage. The average AST level is usually 36 U / L in adults and may be higher in infants and young children.

3. Alkaline phosphatase (ALP). ALP is an enzyme found in the liver and bones and is essential for breaking down proteins. ALP levels higher than normal may indicate liver damage or disease, such as obstruction of the gallbladder, or certain bone diseases. Reliable Source of ALPT because their bones are growing. Pregnancy can also increase ALP levels. The average ALP range for adults is usually 20–140 IU / Reliable Source.

4. Albumin and total protein. Albumin is one of the many proteins produced in the liver. Your body needs these proteins to fight infections and perform other functions. Low levels of albumin and a total protein content may indicate liver damage or disease.Admine testAdd side effects of this test may indicate that your liver is not functioning properly. This occurs in diseases such as cirrhosis, malnutrition, and cancer.

The normal range of albumin is 35–50 grams per liter (g / L). However, a decrease in albumin may also be the result of malnutrition, kidney disease, infections, and inflammation.

5. Bilirubin. Bilirubin is a substance produced during the normal breakdown of red blood cells. Bilirubin passes through the liver and is excreted in the liver. High levels of bilirubin (jaundice) may indicate liver damage or disease or certain types of anemia. High bilirubin levels with high ALT or AST may suggest hepatitis or hepatitis C.

6. Gamma-glutamyltransferase (GGT). GGT is an enzyme in the blood. Higher levels than normal may indicate damage to the liver or bile duct.

7. L-lactate dehydrogenase (LD). LD is an enzyme found in the liver. High levels may indicate liver damage but may be exacerbated in many other diseases.

8. Prothrombin Time (PT). PT is the time it takes your blood to break down. Increased PT may indicate liver damage but may also increase if you are taking certain blood thinners, such as warfarin.

Thyroid function Test

The thyroid gland is in front of your neck just below the apple of your Adam. It is made up of two lobes, on both sides of the trachea, connected by a small thyroid bridge called the isthmus. The thyroid gland produces two key hormones in the blood. One of them is thyroxine, which contains four atoms of iodine and is commonly called T4. This is converted to tri-iodothyronine (T3), which contains three atoms of iodine. It is T3 that works biologically and controls the digestion of food in your body.

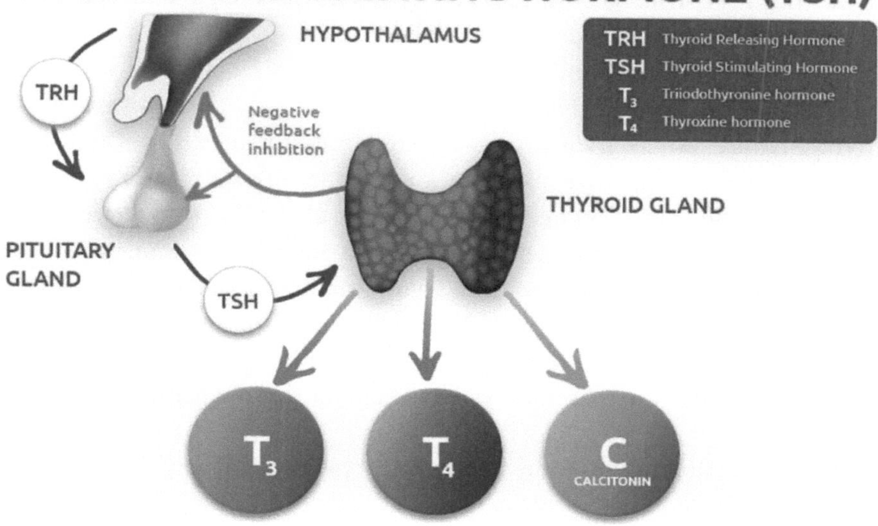

Thyroid Stimulating Hormone

- If the TSH level is above the reference range, T4 blood will be measured.
- If the TSH level is below the distance reference, blood T4 and T3 blood will be measured.

A blood sample is taken from a vein in the arm and sent to a laboratory for analysis. Usually the 'free' or active component of T4 and T3 is measured (i.e., FT4 and FT3). Laboratories use grade reference to compare blood test results with those of normal health. The most common categories of reference to healthy adults are:

Check From Units

TSH 0.4 to 4. 0 mU / l (millimeters per liter)

FT4 9.0 to 25.0 pmol / l (picomoles liter)

FT3 3.5 to 7.8 pmol / l (picomoles liter)

Diagnose thyroid disorders

TSH and FT4

If the TSH level is high and the FT4 effect is low this raises an underactive thyroid (hypothyroidism) that needs treatment.

If the TSH level is low and the FT4 effect is high this raises the hyperthyroidism that needs treatment.

If the TSH level is slightly increased but the FT4 level is still within the normal reference range this is called subclinical hypothyroidism or mild thyroid failure. It may gradually develop into full or clinical hypothyroidism over many years; further examination of the thyroid gland will help determine the risk. Some people with subclinical hypothyroidism, especially those with a TSH level greater than 10mU / l or women who are trying to conceive, may benefit from levothyroxine treatment.

Low TSH with low FT4 may be the result of pituitary gland failure (secondary hypothyroidism caused by hypopituitarism) or a response to any important disease that does not involve your thyroid gland.

FT3

This is usually only used in testing for hyperthyroidism or assessing its severity.

Thyroid antibodies

If the first results of a thyroid test show signs of a thyroid problem and if there is a suspicion of autoimmune disease, one or more thyroid antibody tests may be stopped. Antibody tests are used to confirm the diagnosis of autoimmune thyroid diseases. Some people will be tested for more than one type of thyroid antibody.

In people with subclinical thyroid disease the presence of antibodies may indicate that a person may continue to have a full-blown thyroid disease in the future, but that treatment is not yet necessary.

Immune system can also be present in people who do not have thyroid disease.

CHAPTER VIII

Immunochemistry

Immunochemistry

- Structure & functions of immunoglobulin
- Investigations & interpretation- ELISA

ANTIBODIES/IMMUNOGLOBULINS

Antibodies are globulin proteins (immunoglobulins) that will produce in response to antigens. Immunoglobulins are also known as antibodies. They are amazingly diverse and direct in their ability to see external structures. Basically, lymphocytes are the only cells that make up an antibody molecule. In addition, the immune system makes up about 20 percent of the protein in our blood plasma. In total, there are three types of globulin in the blood, namely alpha, beta, and gamma. The immune system is gamma globulins.

Functions

The most important function of the immune system is to provide protection against germs. Some of the important functions of the immune system are:

- Reduce the risk of germs by eliminating toxins and viruses.
- They make the bacteria easier to phagocytosed, and, acting as a complement, the immune system will prevent the attachment of bacteria to the inferior mucosal areas.

STRUCTURE OF ANTIBODIES/IMMUNOGLOBULINS

Immunoglobulins glycoprotein comprises four polypeptide chains: two identical light (L) and two identical heavy chains (H). In addition, the L and H chains are divided into flexible and permanent circuits. The simplest and heaviest terms refer to molecular weight. Heavy chains are long and light chains are short. Light chains have a molecular weight of about 25,000 Da and heavy chains weigh 50-70,000 Da cells.

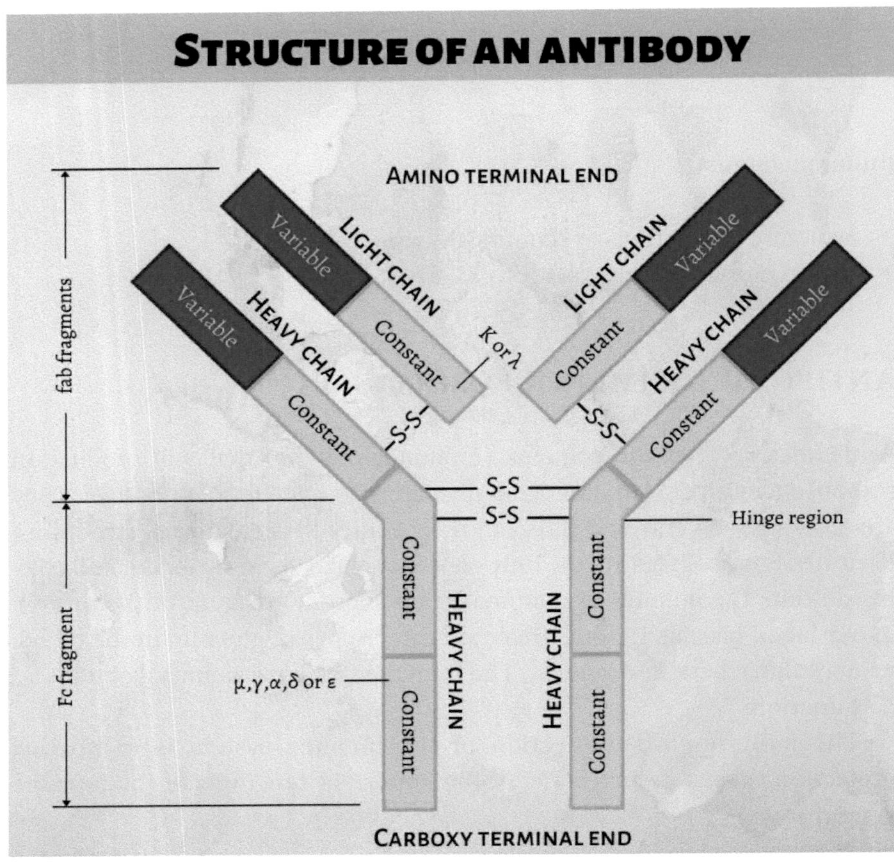

A simple antibody molecule has the structure 'Y' or 'T' which is the most visible element of the immunoglobulin structure. All antibody molecules share the same basic structural features but show significant variability in regions that include antigens. Because the core structure of each antibody molecule contains two heavy chains and two light chains, each antibody molecule has two antigen binding sites.

Immunoglobulin (Ig) domain

Both light chains and heavy chains contain a series of repetitive, homologous units. Each unit has 110 amino acid residues in length, which wrap independently in a globular motif called Ig. The Ig domain consists of two layers of β-pleated sheet, each layer composed of three to five strands of parallel-resistant polypeptide chain. However, the number of fibers in each sheet varies between individual proteins.

Within the wires, hydrophobic and hydrophilic amino acids interact and their side chains are aligned with the sheet plane.

Heavy chains of immunoglobulins

The immunoglobulin molecule has two heavy chains. Each heavy chain contains 420-440 amino acids. Also, each heavy chain binds to a simple chain with disulfide bonds and noncovalent bonds.

Sequence of fixed heavy-chain circuits falls into five basic patterns. The following five basic sequences are named after the Greek alphabet and are:

mu (mu)

δ (delta)

γ (gamma)

ε (epsilon)

alpha (alpha).

The heavy chains of a given antibody molecule determine the stage of that virus. For example, IgM contains μ (mu), IgG contains γ (gamma), IgA contains α (alpha), IgD contains δ (delta), and IgE contains u -ε (epsilon). heavy chains. These heavy chains are structurally and antigenically different in each class of immunoglobulin.

In addition, heavy chains exist in two different ways at the end of the carboxyl-terminal. One type of heavy chain strengthens the immune system to bind plasma to the B lymphocytes and another
the form is hidden when associated with Ig light light chains.

Light chain

The immunoglobulin molecule has two light chains. Each light chain contains 220–240 amino acids. In addition, the light chain attaches to a heavy chain with a disulfide bond. Unlike heavy chains, light chains have structural and chemical properties similar to all classes of immunoglobulins. There are two types:

K (kappa), once

λ (lambda).

Each immunoglobulin has two chains kap (kappa) or two λ (lambda) but never two. In humans, about 60% of antibody molecules have K (kappa) light chains and about 40% have λ light chains. The chains of K (kappa) and λ (lambda) are present in human serum in a ratio of 2: 1.

Each light chain includes one V (flexible) Ig domain and one Ig (permanent) domain Ig. Mutable regions divide the immune system into a single clone of B cells and the immune system to other clones.

Variable and constant region

Each polypeptide chain of the immunoglobulin molecule contains an amino-terminal component and a carboxy-terminal component. Part of the amino terminal is called the variable region (region V) and the carboxy-terminal part is called the stable region (region C).

The flexible regions of both the light and heavy chain are responsible for antigen binding while the stable site of the heavy chain is responsible for various biologic functions. For example, complete activation and bind to cell surface receptors.

Constant region

A fixed circuit (C) is a carboxyl-terminal molecule. It contains the basic sequence of amino acids. The fixed circuit of the light chain has no biological function while the fixed area of the heavy chain is responsible for opening the complement, binding to the cell surface receptors, transferring the placenta, and many other biological functions.

In addition, C-domain domains are different from the antigen binding site and do not participate in antigen recognition.

Variable region

The flexible region contains 100-110 amino acids at the end of the amino-terminal. This region is different for each class of immunoglobulins. Basically, the flexible regions of both the L and H chains have three amino acid sequences that are highly flexible (hypervariable) at the end of the amino-terminal that forms an antigen-binding site.

Flexible loops like fingers from each flexible domain, three fingers from a heavy chain and three fingers from a series of light come together to form a site that binds to the antigen.

These antigen binding sites are responsible for the special binding of antibodies and antigens.

Fab fragments (fragment antigen-binding)

It is a region in antibody binding to antigens. It combines one fixed domain and one heavy domain each with a light chain. These domains form a site that binds to the antigen, at the end of the amino monomer terminal.

Fc fragments (fragment crystallizable)

The Fc region is the antibody tail region that interacts with cell surface receptors called Fc receptors and other proteins of the corresponding system. This structure allows the immune system to produce antibodies.

The immune system, also known as immunoglobulins, is of five types.

IgG, IgA, IgM, IgD, IgE

IgG

Each IgG molecule has two L chains and two H chains linked to disulfide bonds. It weighs 1,50,000 Da cells and has a lifespan of 23 days (the longest of all immunoglobulins). It is a divalent molecule because it has two identical binding sites for antigens.

IgG is the most abundant class of immunoglobulins in serum, comprising about 80% of the total serum immunoglobulin. Depending on the antigenic differences in H chains and the number and location of disulfide bonds, there are four categories of IgG, namely: IgG1, IgG2, IgG3, and IgG4. They are calculated according to their decrease in serum concentration.

Basically, IgG1 makes up the majority (65%) of total IgG. The IgG2 antibody is targeted at polysaccharide antigens and is an important protection against coagulated bacteria.

IgG is the only antibody to cross the placenta and, therefore, is the most abundant immunoglobulin in newborns. This is an example of the immune system being developed because IgG is produced by the mother, not the fetus.

Functions

1. IgG1, IgG3, and IgG4 are the only potent immunoglobulins that cross the placenta. Therefore, they play a vital role in protecting the developing fetus from disease.
2. IgG3, IgG1, and IgG2, respectively, are effective in complementary function.
3. It participates in the rainy season, the associated repair, and the elimination of toxins and viruses.
4. It binds to microorganisms and facilitates the phagocytosis process of microorganisms.

IgA

IgA is the second largest serum immunoglobulin, which comprises approximately 10-15% of serum immunoglobulin. Lifespan of 6-8 days. In addition, it is the main immunoglobulin in secretions such as colostrum, saliva, tears, and respiratory tract, intestines, and the excretory tract. In addition, IgA comes in two forms:

Serum IgA: It is present in serum and is a monomeric molecule with a molecular weight of 60,000 Da. It has two subclasses, IgA1 and IgA2.

secretory IgA: dimer or tetramer and contains J-chain polypeptide. Secretory IgA is a major immunoglobulin present in external secretions, such as breast milk, saliva, tears, and bronchial, genitourinary, and digestive tract.

Functions

1. It protects the mucous membranes from microbial pathogens. Because it is polymeric, secret IgA can link major antigens with multiple epitopes.
2. Secretory IgA protects newborns from infection during the first month of life. Because the baby's immune system is not fully developed, breastfeeding plays an important role in maintaining the health of newborns.
3. Secretory IgA has been shown to provide an important line of defense against bacteria and viruses.

IgM

IgM makes up about 5-8% of total serum immunoglobulins. It is a heavy molecule weighing from 900,000 to 1,000,000 Da. It lasts half 5 days. IgM antibodies are short-lived and disappear prematurely compared to IgG. The presence of IgM antibody in the serum, therefore, indicates a recent infection.

IgM is the main immunoglobulin that produces in the early response. It exists as a monomer on the surface of almost all B cells while in the serum, exists as a pentamer, composed of five subunoglobulin subunits and one J chain molecule. In comparison, it works much better than IgG in activating a complement.

Because the pentamer has 10 antigen binding sites, it is an immunoglobulin that is very effective in binding, co-activating (activating), and other immune responses.

Functions

1. IgM provides protection from blood attacks by microbial pathogens. IgM Immune Deficiency Syndrome is associated with septicemia.
2. IgM is not transported through the placenta; therefore, the presence of IgM in the fetus or newborn indicates intrauterine infection. Therefore, the presence of IgM antibodies in serum helps to diagnose congenital diseases, such as syphilis, rubella, toxoplasmosis, etc.

IgD

IgD forms less than 1% of serum immunoglobulins. It is a monomer with a molecular weight of 180,000 Da. The half-life of IgD is only 2-3 days. is present in the surface of many B lymphocytes and in small amounts in serum. Both IgD and IgM act as antigen receptor receptors. The role of IgD in vaccination continues to be elusive.

Functions

begins the body's immune responses. However, its exact function is not known.

IgE

IgE forms less than 1% of total immunoglobulin. It weighs 1,90,000 Da cells and a half-life of 2-3 days. Unlike other heat-resistant immunoglobulins, IgE is a heat-absorbing protein and does not easily work at 56 ° C for 1 hour.

It is present in serum at very low concentrations (0.002%). It is most commonly found in the lining of the respiratory tract and intestines. Although, IgE is present in trace amounts to normal serum, people with allergic reactivity have significantly increased IgE levels and may be seen in external secretions.

In addition, IgE does not repair the complement and does not cross the placenta.

Investigations & interpretation- ELISA

ELISA

ELISA is a basic diagnostic test, known as an enzyme-linked immunosorbent assay (also called EIA: Enzyme Immunoassay) that is performed to detect and measure antibodies, hormones, peptides, and proteins in the blood.

Blood protein antibodies are produced in response to a specific antigen. It is helpful to check the presence of antibodies in the body, if there are certain infectious diseases.

ELISA is a unique analysis compared to other antimicrobial tests as it reveals the quantitative effects and separation of the indirect and indirect interactions that occur with successive binding in solid surfaces, usually a polystyrene multiwell plate.

Types Of ELISA

ELISA tests can be classified into three types depending upon the different methods used for binding between antigen and antibodies, namely:

1. Indirect ELISA – Antigen is coated to the microtiter well
2. Sandwich ELISA – Antibody is coated on the microtiter well
3. Competitive ELISA – Microtiter well which is antigen-coated is filled with the antigen-antibody mixture.

ELISA tests can be divided into three types depending on the different methods used to bind between antigens and antibodies, namely:

1. Indirect ELISA - Antigen is well integrated with microtiter
2. Sandwich ELISA - The antibody is firmly attached to the microtiter
3. Competitive ELISA - A well-anti-coated Microtiter packed with antigen-antibody compound.

Indirect ELISA

Indirect ELISA detects the presence of antibody in the sample.

1. The antigen is attached to the microtitre plate sources.
2. A sample containing antibodies was added to antigen-covered wells to bind to the antigen.
3. The free antibodies are washed away and the antigen-antibody complex is obtained by adding a second antibody to the enzyme that can combine with the main antibody.
4. All free second antibodies are washed. A specific substrate is added that gives the product a color.
5. The absorption of a colored product is measured by spectrophotometry.

Sandwich ELISA

Sandwich ELISA helps determine the presence of antigen in the sample.

1. The microtitre source is covered with antibody.
2. A sample containing antigen was added to the source and washed to remove free antigens.
3. Then a second enzyme-linked antibody, which binds to another epitope in the antigen is added. The well is washed to release free antibodies.

4. An enzyme-specific substrate is added to the plate to form a colored, non-abrasive product.

Competitive ELISA

ELISA competition helps to find the target antigen concentration in the sample.

- Microtitre sources are associated with antigen.
- Antibodies are placed in a solution containing antigen.
- Antigen-antibody complex solution is added to microtitre sources. The well is then washed to remove loose tissue.
- The more antigen in the sample, the more free the immune system available to interact with the antigen, which is covered in the source.
- A second antibody attached to the enzyme was added to determine the number of key antibodies present in the source.
- The focus is then determined by spectrophotometry.

Principle of ELISA

ELISA works by the principle that certain antibodies bind the target antigen and detect the presence and number of binding antigens. To increase the sensitivity and accuracy of the test, the plate should be covered with highly compatible antibodies. ELISA can provide useful estimates of antigen-antibody concentration.

ELISA Procedure

ELISA is one of the easiest blood tests that can be done. It is fast, quick and requires a patient blood sample. The entire ELISA process is outlined below.

1. The antibody is attached to a surface polystyrene plate that is strong and attractive or related to germs, other antibodies and hormones.
2. The antigen-associated microtiter is supplemented with this antigen-antibody compound after which free antibodies are released by washing.
3. A second antibody corresponding to the main antibody is added which is usually combined with an enzyme.
4. Free enzyme-linked antibodies are released by washing the plate.
5. Finally, a substrate was added. The substrate is converted by an enzyme to form a pigmented product, which can be measured by spectrophotometry.

6. The HCG protein that indicates pregnancy is detected by ELISA. A combination of a blood or urine sample and pure HCG-binding enzyme are added to the system. If HCG is not present in the test sample, then only the linked enzyme binds to the solid state.
7. The more the object of interest, the more reaction occurs and the less of the linked enzyme binds to a solid surface. This reaction is usually indicated by a change in the color of the solution.

Diseases That Can Be Diagnosed Using ELISA

ELISA can be used to detect some of the following conditions:

- Ebola
- Dangerous anemia
- AIDS
- Rotavirus
- Lyme disease
- Syphilis
- Toxoplasmosis
- Zika virus
- Carcinoma of epithelial cells

Advantages Of ELISA

The following are some of the benefits of the ELISA strategy:

1. The results collected from ELISA provide an accurate diagnosis of a specific disease as two antibodies are used.
2. It can be performed on complex samples as the antigen does not need to be purified in order to be detected.
3. It is very responsive as direct and indirect analysis methods can be performed.
4. It is a fast test, producing fast results.
5. The potential findings of ELISA vary from quantity, semi-quantitative, standard curve, quality, model curve models etc.
6. It is also easier to perform a simple procedure compared to other tests that require the presence of radioactive material.

Applications of ELISA

ELISA applications are discussed below:

1. The presence of antibodies and antigens in the sample can be determined.
2. It is used in the food industry to detect any food allergies that are present.
3. Determining serum antibody saturation in viral load testing.

During an outbreak, to assess the spread of the disease, e.g. during the recent outbreak of COVID-19, rapid diagnostic tools are used to detect the presence of antibodies in a blood sample.

University Question Papers(2021)

July 2021

In univeraity exam biochemistry paper contains 30 marks out of 75 marks. This is a combine paper of Nutrition and Biochemistry

1. Regulation of cholestrol biosynthesis
2. TCA cycle
3. Classification of antibodies
4. Fat soluble vitamins
5. Enzyme inhibition
6. Lipoprotein and their functions .

University Question Paper 2021

January 2021

1. Regulation of blood glucose.
2. Active transport system across cell membrane.
3. clinical importance of estimation of bilirubin
4. Urea cycle
5. Structure of immunoglobulins
6. Atherosclerosis.

University Question Paper(2020)

1. Regulation of blood glucose.
2. pentose phosphate pathway.
3. Immune Response.
4. Water soluble vitamins.
5. Diagnostic significance of enzyme.
6. Buffers

University Question Paper 2019

1. Regulation of glycolysis
2. Glycogenolysis
3. LDL
4. Competitive enzyme inhibition
5. Vitamin K deficiency
6. Buffers.

University Question Paper(2018)

1. Regulation of enzyme activity
2. ATP synthesis
3. Hemoglobin F
4. Phenylketonuria
5. Transamination
6. Types of immunoglobulins and their structure

Printed by Libri Plureos GmbH in Hamburg,
Germany